D0458253

WHAT *ARE* YOU?

P E A R L F U Y O G A S K I N S

Henry Holt and Company / New York

WHAT ARE YOU?

VOICES OF MIXED-RACE YOUNG PEOPLE

Henry Holt and Company, Inc.
Publishers since 1866
175 Fifth Avenue
New York, New York 10010
www.henryholt.com

Henry Holt is a registered trademark
of Henry Holt and Company, Inc.
Copyright © 1999 by Pearl Fuyo Gaskins. All rights reserved.
Published in Canada by Fitzhenry & Whiteside Ltd.,
195 Allstate Parkway, Markham, Ontario L3R 4T8.

Library of Congress Cataloging-in-Publication Data
What are you?: voices of mixed-race young people / edited by Pearl Fuyo Gaskins.
p.   cm.
Includes bibliographical references and index.
Summary: Many young people of racially mixed backgrounds discuss their
feelings about family relationships, prejudice, dating, personal identity, and other
issues.
1. Racially mixed people—United States—Interviews—Juvenile literature.
2. Young adults—United States—Interviews—Juvenile literature.
3. Teenagers—United States—Interviews—Juvenile literature.
4. United States—Race relations—Case studies—Juvenile literature.
[1. Racially mixed people. 2. Ethnicity. 3. Race relations.]   I. Gaskins,
Pearl Fuyo.
E184.A1W385   1999   973—dc21   98-37381

ISBN-13: 978-0-8050-5968-7 / ISBN-10: 0-8050-5968-7
First Edition—1999
Printed in the United States of America on acid-free paper. ∞
7 8 9 10

Permission for the use of the following is gratefully acknowledged:
"Bill of Rights for Racially Mixed People" is from The Multiracial Experience: Racial
Borders as the New Frontier, *by Maria P. P. Root, p. 7, copyright © 1993, 1994,*
1997 by Maria P. P. Root. Reprinted by permission of Sage Publications, Inc.

"On Being Blackanese" was originally published in Interracial Voice *magazine,*
April 1996 (www.webcom.com/~intvoice).

All poems, essays, and extracts not specifically cited here
are used by permission of their authors.

TO MY LATE FATHER, ALBERT GASKINS,
AND MY MOTHER, IKUKO GASKINS

I've wanted to write this book since I was fifteen years old. Many people helped to make my dream come true. First and foremost, I'd like to thank the eighty young people who generously shared their poetry, essays, and life stories. I couldn't quote every one of them by name, but each contributed a sliver of experience that made this book better. Their enthusiasm sustained me.

I'd also like to thank the many experts who shared their valuable knowledge, insights, and wisdom. Their work guided me in my research. They include: Maria P. P. Root, Cindy Nakashima, George Kich, Teresa Kay Williams, Reginald Daniel, Jonathan Marks, Mark Nathan Cohen, Anton Hart, Christine Iijima Hall, Carla Bradshaw, Amy Iwasaki Mass, Lynda Field, and Ramona Douglass. I am especially grateful to Dr. Root for allowing me to include her powerful "Bill of Rights for Racially Mixed People" and Reginald Daniel for his comments on parts of the manuscript.

On the publishing end, I owe a big thanks to Marc Aronson, my editor at Henry Holt, for giving me the opportunity to create this book and perhaps make a difference in the lives of some racially mixed young people and their families. Marc encouraged me to follow my vision for this book and deftly guided me along the way. I am also grateful to Ellen Clyne and Barbara Kouts for putting my proposal in Marc's hands, and Lloyd Jassin for his legal advice.

Tracking down these mixed-race young people wouldn't have been possible without the help of Greg Mayeda and Hapa Issues Forum, Charles Byrd and his *Interracial Voice* online magazine, Rahsaan and Dainie of FAMLEE, Irene Carr of the Association of MultiEthnic Americans (AMEA), and my friends Angela Elliott and

Karen Watanabe. Kat Wade contributed several beautiful photographs.

I was extremely fortunate in finding many bright and capable people to assist me. Ann Jacobs, Debbie Isselin, and Nancy Tonachio of A Adel Transcribers in South Orange, New Jersey, did a wonderful job of transcribing most of the taped interviews. Tatsu Yamato came up with some interesting Web sites for the resources section. I couldn't have asked for a better assistant than Jenny Ho in the final weeks before my manuscript was due. Karen Brown, the Wednesday Night Group, and Lisa Sattler helped me stay strong.

The advice and encouragement I received from Mark Bregman and Renee Glaser, colleagues at Scholastic, were vital. I want to acknowledge my family—especially Sarah and Lam—and my friends for their tolerance of my self-absorption over the past months.

Most of all, I'd like to thank my generous and loving husband, Randy Brockway, for understanding why this book was important to me and for supporting the sacrifices we both had to make so that I could complete it.

ME

What are you anyway?
Black? White? Mixed? Latina? Native American?
Mulatto? Caribbean? Puerto Rican? Gringa?
Middle Eastern? Central American? Venezuelan?
Italian? Greek? Biracial? Cape Verdean? Spanish?
Cuban? Irish? Trigueña? Jewish? Hispanic? Morena?
Multiracial? Colombian? Eastern European? African?
Mestizo? Brazilian? . . .

I'm all of the above because you *think* I am
(depending on the clothes I'm wearing, the company
I'm keeping, the language I'm speaking, the food
I'm eating, the style of my hair, the shade of my
skin, the country I'm in), and I'm none of the above.

What am I?
I'm a question. I'm an answer.
I'm a resister of racial classifications,
A defier of ethnic designations,
A list of possible labels,
And a navigator of niches that don't quite fit.
I'm a petitioner for no more pigeonholing,
Who loves to keep you guessing.
I'm a medley, a mixture,
A collage of colors,
A blended body shifting shades,
A cultural chameleon
Of ambiguous ancestry and hybrid heritage.

I'm creator of my own category,
I'm inventor of my own identity.

I'm mixed, but I'm *not* mixed up.
I'm not about denying a part of me.
I'm not about trying to pass.
I'm no sellout, no traitor,
No wanna-be, no mutt.
I'm no tragedy, and no exotic other.
. . . If anything, I'm just another hue of you.
I'm not about confusion
(unless you mean other people's confusion).
I'm not about anomaly or impurity,
About halfness or being in between.
I'm no less of one thing than I am of another.
I'm no poster child for interracial harmony,
No model for miscegenated humanity.
I'm not about messy mingling,
And I'm not what's meant by the melting pot.
I'm no jungle-fever rainbow baby,
No icon for interbreeding.
I'm not about trying to be better than anyone else,
Or trying to be different.
What *I'm* about is being *all* of what I am . . .
Nothing more, nothing less, nothing else.

I'm a black + white + I don't know what else =
both/neither/other, "half" transracially adopted,
descendant of people I've never met. A freckled,
brown-skinned, curly/straight/frizzy brown-haired
(with some black, blond, and orange thrown in),

ME

German-American raised, Spanish-speaking gringa
and multicolorful part-time expatriate. I'm mixed.
What I *am* is *ME* ☑.

By SARA B. BUSDIECKER, copyright © 1997
Age: Twenty-six
East Lansing, Michigan
Sara is biracial and adopted.
Her parents are German-American.

CONTENTS

WHAT *ARE* YOU?

INTRODUCTION

It was April 24, 1997. Golfing phenom Tiger Woods and his father, Earl, were guests on the ever-popular *Oprah Winfrey* show. Just a week earlier, Tiger, then only twenty-one, made sports history by becoming the youngest golfer and the first "African-American" to win the prestigious Masters golf tournament. His victory by an incredible twelve strokes broke course records and left many of the world's best golfers in the dust.

Within hours Tiger became the biggest and most sought-after celebrity on the planet, and a role model to millions of kids. Golf, viewed by many as a stuffy sport played by rich white men, was suddenly cool. Tiger could do no wrong—except for one thing. He refused to label himself as simply African-American. He was more than black, he told Oprah Winfrey, and proudly claimed his multiple heritages. "Growing up, I came up with this name—I'm a *Cablinasian*," said Tiger, whose father is African-American, American Indian, and Chinese, and whose mother is Thai, Chinese, and white. Cablinasian, he explained, was shorthand for Caucasian, black, Indian, and Asian.

Asked by Winfrey if it bothered him to be labeled only African-American, Tiger said it did. When he had to identify his racial background by checking off one box on school forms, he usually picked "African-American and Asian, because those are the two households I was raised under."

Tiger's racial identity immediately became national news. Some journalists and sportscasters were obviously amused and reported it as some strange eccentricity of the boy genius of golf. "Cablin—what?" they cracked. But many African-Americans were not amused. They quickly denounced him: "He's black. He's denying his blackness." "He doesn't know who he is." "He's confused." For a while, the controversy over Tiger's racial identity threatened to eclipse his amazing achievement.

The fact that Americans are obsessed with race and racial categorization wasn't news to me. As a racially mixed person, I have been asked, "What do you call yourself?" "What *are* you?" or "Where are you from?" countless times by curious and sometimes obnoxious people, including a high school music teacher, dance partners at nightclubs, and strangers on the subway.

Like Tiger, I've scratched my head over racial-identification questions on school forms and standardized tests that read "Check one box." As I was growing up, I learned that in the eyes of many people I am the product of a relationship that wasn't supposed to happen.

My parents met in Tokyo, Japan, and married on October 5, 1955. My mother's Japanese family was against the marriage because my father, who died in 1988, was not Japanese—he was an American and he was white. My mother's father never forgave her. He disinherited her. At that time, my mother tells me, Japanese women who married American servicemen were thought to be bar girls and prostitutes, an unfair and demeaning stereotype.

My parents came to the United States. It was 1956, and interracial marriage—especially between blacks and whites—was against the law in many states. It wasn't until 1967, when I was ten years old, that the U.S. Supreme Court ruled that state laws forbidding interracial marriage were unconstitutional.

Of course, as a child, I wasn't aware of the existence of anti-miscegenation laws. But I learned in other ways that many Americans viewed interracial relationships as unnatural and wrong, and that being the product of such a relationship and also being a person of Asian-American ancestry was a double whammy.

I was called a "Jap" and a "Chink" by black and white kids in grade school. I dreaded the anniversary of Pearl Harbor in history class because someone always made a crack about "those sneaky Japs." And most of all, I noticed that my mother, an Asian woman, was someone whom others thought they could treat with less respect. People behind counters were impatient with her. "Don't you understand English?" one woman sniped. The tone was unmistakable, even to an eight-year-old.

For me, being picked on wasn't the biggest problem—being ignored was. As a racially mixed person, I felt invisible and alone. I remember looking forward to grocery shopping at the nearby military base, because that was the only time I saw families that looked like mine and racially mixed kids like me. Interracial families—or people of color, for that matter—were never pictured in school textbooks or seen eating dinner together in TV sitcoms and commercials.

When interracial relationships were portrayed in novels and movies, the story and the relationship ended predictably with death, insanity, or abandonment. From *West Side Story* and *Madame Butterfly* to *Show Boat* and *South Pacific,* the message was easy to read: Don't make this mistake. These relationships are doomed. When I was growing up, the only mixed-race people I remember seeing on TV were the Indian "half-breeds" who stole horses on Saturday afternoon Westerns. The good guys in the white hats despised them even more than they hated the full-blooded Indians.

Adolescence was the time when I wrestled most deeply with the issues of race and racial identity. It was the mid-1970s. I was living in Vallejo, which was then a small, predominantly white working-class city sandwiched between the northern reaches of San Francisco Bay and the California foothills.

The militancy of the 1960s was a recent memory, and bold, loud displays of racial pride were fashionable. People plastered their heritages on the back windows of their cars: red, black, and green "Afro" stickers, Mexican and Italian flags. Not wanting to be left out, I slapped a Japanese flag on the hatchback window of my mom's Ford Pinto. I hammered metal studs that spelled out "yellow is mellow" down the side of my jeans.

For myself and many of my peers, racial identification determined the music we listened to, the clothes and hairstyles we wore, the slang we used, who our friends were, and whom we dated. As teenagers trying to carve out identities for ourselves, we found in race and ethnicity instant self-definition and a sense of group belonging. And for many nonwhite teens, this ethnic awareness was a way of coping with the racism they experienced in their day-to-day lives.

It was a tough time and place to be biracial. Racial purity was cool, being mixed was not. I wasn't white enough and I wasn't nonwhite enough. There were no positive words to describe what I was or what group I belonged to.

It wasn't until I was a sophomore in college that I found those words—*biracial, Amerasian, Eurasian*. I discovered that I was not alone; there were others like me. In fact, people of mixed racial heritage had made numerous contributions to this country. They included great people, such as abolitionist and human rights leader Frederick Douglass, ornithologist John James Audubon, sculptor Isamu Noguchi, and prima ballerina Maria Tallchief. I learned that racially mixed people were acknowledged in other places—Brazil, Hong Kong, and Indonesia, to name a few—and that there were whole communities of them all over the world.

Fast-forward to the 1990s. The number of interracial marriages in the United States has skyrocketed over the past thirty years. By

1990, the Census Bureau reported that one in twenty-five married couples was interracial. In California, the figure was even higher: one in ten. Demographers describe a biracial baby boom. The number of children, age eighteen and under, who live with their interracially married parents has more than quadrupled since I was a teenager. Demographer Reynolds Farley of New York City's Russell Sage Foundation estimates that these young people currently number at least four million. About a quarter of them are of black and white parentage, but the majority—about 70 percent—come from homes where one parent is white and the other is either Asian-American, Hispanic, or Native American.

Biracial people are suddenly a presence. Mixed-race children toddle alongside their parents on the streets of New York City, San Francisco, and Minneapolis. Racially ambiguous models populate ads for Calvin Klein and Benetton. The pages of *People, Spin,* and *Sports Illustrated* are filled with multiracial celebrities, from singer Mariah Carey and actress-model Halle Berry to Yankee shortstop Derek Jeter and musician Sean Lennon. After Tiger Woods burst into the spotlight, some journalists reported that being racially mixed has become chic, even cool.

I'm now an adult and a journalist who writes articles for an educational magazine for teenagers. Every so often I receive letters from readers who are racially mixed. But being perceived as cool is not what they write about. A girl from Nevada says she was called "half-breed" and "Oreo" by black teenagers. A boy from Tennessee was rejected by white relatives who couldn't accept his African-American heritage. The pain and loneliness between the lines take me back to my own teenage years.

I decided to create a book for them—the book I wish I'd had when I was a teenager. It would have to be empowering. It would have to be a forum for mixed-race young people to share their experiences and validate their feelings. It would have to educate others—parents, teachers, and young people who are not racially mixed.

So, in late 1995, I began to interview people. I cast a wide net—I networked through family and friends, contacted interracial family groups, sent flyers to universities, and posted bulletins on the Internet. By 1998, I had talked to eighty racially mixed young people, meeting with as many of them as I could. They were between the ages of fourteen and twenty-eight; most were eighteen to twenty-two. They came from all over the United States—from cities, suburbs, and small towns, and from places as diverse as Hawaii, New Jersey, and Alabama.

The race and ethnicity of the people I talked to vary as well and reflect the many ways of being racially mixed. Most of them are biracial; that is, their parents are an interracial couple. Others, though, take pride in a mixed ancestry that goes back generations. Also, while many of them used the label "mixed race" or "multiracial" to describe themselves, some were more comfortable sticking to traditional racial categories such as black, Asian-American, or Indian. Some individualists refused to label themselves at all.

This book includes poetry, essays, and portions of interviews with approximately forty-five of these people. The words in this book are their words; the interviews were taped, transcribed, and edited for clarity. Whenever possible, participants were sent a copy of their edited interviews to read and given the opportunity to correct any inaccuracies and misinterpretations.

What you see on these pages is the result of this collaboration. And what it illustrates most powerfully is that being racially mixed is a unique and profound experience for many people. No matter what their backgrounds—white and Asian, black and white, and Hispanic and black, for example—they share similar experiences **9** as people who don't fit neatly within the lines of a racially divided society. They cross borders, they straddle lines, they challenge boundaries.

Collectively, their stories paint a portrait of race in America that is both complex and disturbing. They show us that prejudice and intolerance can be found in every group. And that our society's legacy of exploitation and racism—from slavery to the internment of Japanese-Americans—is woven deeply into the fabric of family histories and continues to cause pain today.

But hope can also be found in the voices of the young people you will read about. Most of them were hopeful that positive changes are on the way. The fact that a high-profile person like Tiger Woods could claim a multiracial identity signals a greater acceptance of racially mixed people in our society. The fact that the U.S. government recently revamped its system of racial categorization to allow people to check more than one racial category on federal forms amounts to official recognition of multiracial people—a change that is revolutionary.

Finally, although this book looks primarily at race and ethnicity, I want to emphasize that the young people profiled here have many more dimensions than that. For the most part, they are just like other people their age—they are cheerleaders, college students, teen mothers, jocks, and computer geeks. Growing up, many of them struggled with the problems that plague their peers—divorce, family violence, an alcoholic parent, to name a few. Among them are artists, social scientists, community activists, a mathematician, an award-winning flutist, and others whose interests, talents, and accomplishments are unbounded by race.

NOTES TO THE READER

Each chapter of this book focuses on one theme, or area of common experience, for racially mixed young people. Most people are quoted in several different chapters. If you are interested in a particular person, you can use the index at the back of the book to locate all the pages where he or she speaks.

Essays and some longer profiles called "Snapshots" are sandwiched between chapters. The snapshots enabled me to give longer and richer portraits of several people.

The stories that people told in this book were so powerful and poignant that I tried to stay out of their way as much as possible and let them speak for themselves. But when I thought it might be helpful, I added comments and notes to clarify, define, or make important observations.

In the past ten years, an incredibly provocative body of research about race and mixed-race people has emerged. Historians, sociologists, psychologists, and others—many of whom are racially mixed themselves—have written about the multiracial experience, often stressing its positive and creative aspects. I interviewed many of these experts and wove their helpful insights through the pages of this book.

A few parents didn't want their children's full names used, and in some cases, I disguised identities. Disguised identities are marked with asterisks (*) next to the names. The age given is the age of the person at the time of the interview. The place listed is the primary place where he or she lived as a teenager.

DEFINITIONS

Multiracial, mixed-race, racially mixed: These terms are used interchangeably in this book; they refer to people who can trace their ancestry back to more than one racial group.

Biracial: A first-generation mixed-race person; the product of an interracial relationship between people of two different racial groups (a child of an Asian-American father and a European-American mother, for example).

Multigenerational mixed race: Someone who is the child or descendant of other mixed-race people. People in this group often refer to themselves as multiracial.

Monoracial: A so-called racially "pure" person; someone who identifies himself or herself as white, black, or Asian/Pacific Islander, for example.

Hapa: A Hawaiian word, meaning "foreigner," that has been co-opted by many racially mixed people who have some Asian/Pacific Islander heritage to describe themselves.

BILL OF RIGHTS FOR RACIALLY MIXED PEOPLE

I have the right

    not to justify my existence in this world

    not to keep the races separate within me

    not to be responsible for people's discomfort with my
        physical ambiguity

    not to justify my ethnic legitimacy

I have the right

    to identify myself differently than strangers expect me to
        identify

    to identify myself differently than how my parents identify me

    to identify myself differently than my brothers and sisters

    to identify myself differently in different situations

I have the right

    to create a vocabulary to communicate about being
        multiracial

    to change my identity over my lifetime—and more than once

    to have loyalties and identify with more than one group of
        people

    to freely choose whom I befriend and love

—MARIA P. P. ROOT, Ph.D.

I DON'T THINK OF BEING BIRACIAL AS A BURDEN

KAT WADE

Chela (left) with her best friend, Tanna Larson, who is also biracial.

CHELA DELGADO, fourteen
Oakland, California
Mother: European-American (Scottish)
Father: African-American (Jamaican, East Indian)

My neighborhood is sort of caught between the hills and the flatlands. You walk five minutes in this direction and you get to Fruitvale, and the area's not that great. And you walk five minutes in that direction and you get to the hills, which is a lot nicer. So I live sort of in between.

I have a lot of stuff in me. My mom is pretty much Scottish. My dad is mainly Jamaican; he's a quarter East Indian, and we have a little bit of Portuguese in there somewhere. I can pretty much say that I'm African-American and European-American and Asian-American. But usually I just say I'm mixed black and white—it's the easiest. Sometimes, since I'm so light-skinned, people think I'm white or they think I'm mixed Latina and white.

I remember in second grade I had to fill out one of those things that said "African-American," "Caucasian," "Asian," and whatever. It said "Check one." I said, "Oh, my gosh, which one do I check?"

And my teacher said, "Just put Caucasian," because she thought I was white.

I said, "No, no, I can't, because there's something else."

And she said, "Just put it." And so I just did. And I forgot about that until a few years later and then I was like, "Gosh, that teacher was so stupid."

In my elementary school it wasn't a big thing. It was just natural that I was mixed. But in junior high, people always wanted to know—what was I? In seventh grade, when I was twelve and thirteen, I was sort of still trying to figure it out.

There's been trouble at school—people called me "half-breed" or "zebra" or whatever. At first, I was really shy, and when people would insult me, I didn't know how to defend myself. But now I'll just say, "Shut up. Don't talk to me like that."

At my school the white kids get harassed a lot, because it's really a minority school—there's mostly black kids, then Asian, Latino, white, and then biracial. So I've been asked, "What are you?" And when I say I'm biracial, a lot of times people will treat me better. It makes me really mad because it shouldn't matter. Even if they did treat me better, it's still the same principle— you're treating me differently because of my race, and screw you; it shouldn't make a difference.

My best friend, Tanna, is biracial. I talked about it with her. I said, "It feels so weird when I'm in a room full of white people and I think, 'Gosh, I'm the only black person in here.' Or when I'm in a room full of black people and I think, 'Gosh, I'm the only white person in here.' " And she could relate to me on that. I actually worked out a philosophy with her. This is our logic: Being biracial isn't hard because we're confused about our racial identity. It's hard because everyone else is confused. The problem isn't us—it's everyone else.

It's not really much of an issue for me anymore. I have biracial friends, and white friends, and Asian friends, and black friends, and we all hang out together. At our school, people mainly hang out with their racial group—like the black kids are over here, and the white kids are over here, and the Asian kids are over here. So it's different for people to see us all together. Most of the time, people don't mess with us.

I know a lot of black kids who think you should keep the race pure. I think that's ridiculous, personally, because we all came from the same place. It's not a dilution to mix. In a hundred years, who knows? Probably half the world will be mixed. They finally started to include "biracial" on those little boxes you check. I used to always have to check "other." There are more and more interracial marriages and there'll be more biracial kids around and they won't have as hard a time. And eventually, it will just be accepted without a second thought.

I think of race as someone's shell. When I say that race doesn't matter, a lot of times people say, "You don't take pride in your race? You don't take pride in who you are?" Yes, I take pride in who I am. I take pride in my heritage. I know my history and I know my heritage, and that, to me, is who I am and where I come from, regardless of the color of my skin.

Heritage does matter. But race and heritage are such different things. In most people's minds, they're the same thing or they're so closely linked that they might as well be the same thing. Race is important because it helps preserve heritage, because it allows you to know more about your heritage.

Being mixed, you really do get the best of both worlds, and sometimes you get the worst—like putting up with people who will insult you because of it and think your parents are immoral or whatever. Sometimes you get teased, and some people say, "How could anyone put a child through that?"

But it's not something my parents put me through. It's something my parents gave to me, and I don't think of being biracial as a burden. It's more like, "Well, yeah, sometimes I have a hard time because some people are ignorant, and it's my job to help them learn about it." You're sort of a trailblazer for others.

I love being biracial just because I love proving people wrong. When someone has a certain stereotype about a black person being this or a white person being that, I blow them out of the water because I do not fit the stereotype of a white Valley girl or a black ghetto girl. I love being able to say, "I don't fit that stereotype—that's wrong." And people have to listen to that because it's absolutely true.

I really love being different and having different experiences than everyone else I know. When you get older, you realize that you don't want to be the same as everyone else. You don't want to fit in.

It used to be a big thing for me—finding where I belonged. Do I belong with black people? Do I belong with white people? Do I belong with biracial people? And now it's like I belong wherever I am. Whatever group I'm in, I can belong there if I want to.

ARE YOU THIS? ARE YOU THAT?

"What nationality are you?"

"Where are you from?"

"Are those colored contacts?"

"Is that a perm?"

"What kind of name is that?"

"What are you?"

If you're racially mixed, you've probably answered questions like these dozens of times. People seem to be obsessed with how we look. Chalk it up to curiosity, right?

It's often more than curiosity that drives people to ask these kinds of questions. Discomfort and anxiety can play a role, observes Maria P. P. Root, a psychologist in Seattle, Washington, who has written extensively about mixed-race issues. "When people experience someone as ambiguous or feel uncertain as to what box or camp to put the person in, it brings out their anxiety." They're thinking, if only subconsciously, "Wait a minute, I'm confused. This doesn't fit. I don't know what box to put you into."

"We are inkblots," says Root, who is racially mixed herself. Inkblots are used in a psychological test in which people's interpretations of the blotches reveal their innermost thoughts. "People see us and they project what they need onto us to make themselves feel comfortable." For example, they may need us to be monoracial or a particular race or ethnicity. They may blurt out assumptions that disclose their prejudices. "We get a window into what their anxieties and fears are."

So the "What are you?" question reveals a lot about the person asking the question. It also says a lot about our society. The frequency with which racially mixed people are asked this question tells us that race is extremely important. It's one of the first things we notice about someone. When people cannot make racial dis-

tinctions and sort people into racial categories they are thrown into a sort of "crisis," concludes Teresa Kay Williams, a sociologist and professor in Asian-American Studies at California State University, Northridge. "The crisis is caused by the contradiction between how people have been trained to understand race and the fact that the multiracial person doesn't fit that scheme."

I'M A LITTLE BIT OF EVERYTHING

YUEN LUI

DEREK SALMOND, fifteen
Auburn, Washington
Mother: European-American
Father: African-American

People often ask me the question, "So what are you anyway?" If I'm having a good day, I won't answer that in a hostile way. But if I'm having a rough day, it gets annoying. You get snappy at people when you realize how often they ask it and how many of them don't really understand.

My answer also depends on how they ask the question. If they ask, "What are you?" I just give them a smart answer. I say, "I'm a human being. Why? What are you?"

Then they go, "Well, what's your nationality?"

I'll tell them African-American and Caucasian-American. Or I will say, "I'm biracial." There's always that look of surprise when you say, "I'm biracial." Most people look at you for a second. I think they either don't comprehend or don't want to comprehend that expression.

Other people look at you and go, "You are?" because everyone automatically assumes that I'm either black, Puerto Rican, or Mexican. And most people are like, "Oh, so your mom's black and your dad's white."

"No, it's vice versa."

It bugs me that most people also automatically assume that my parents must be split up because it's an interracial marriage. They have this idea that biracial children don't live with both of their parents at the same time.

I can't classify myself as anything, nor do I want to. I play in the jazz band at school. I play in a blues band too. I play classical bass. I play water polo, which is mainly a white-dominated sport. I listen to classical music, occasionally alternative music, and rap and country also. I'm a little bit of everything.

I JUST SAY "NATIVE AMERICAN"

INDIA,* twenty-three
Indiana
Mother: Native American, Black, White
Father: Native American, Black, White

I was eating dinner in the dorm at a table full of people, and all of a sudden, one of the guys I knew came up. He saw me and said, "India, what *are* you?" That totally caught me off guard, and

I was embarrassed. I just wasn't expecting it in front of all those people. It made me feel so different from everyone else.

I get asked what I am a lot. I usually just answer that I am mixed. But then that isn't enough of an answer for most people; they want to know details. So I say, "I'm black, white, and Indian," and people always want to know more. "Which parent is what?" Then I have the difficulty of explaining that both of my parents are mixed.

So now, if I don't feel like explaining, I just say "Native American." Most of the time, people are very happy with hearing that response.

MY ETHNIC BACKGROUND IS A HIGHLY PERSONAL THING

OLAN MILLS

CHRISTY MATTE, twenty-five
Lowell, Massachusetts
Mother: European-American
Father: European-American
Biological Father: African-American

I have had people walk up to me out of the blue and say, "What are you?" Like I'll be shopping and somebody will watch me for a few minutes and then come up and ask.

I've had people go through these long lists: "Are you this?" "Are you that?" "Are you this?" I just think it's rude. I can't imagine **23** walking up to a complete stranger and asking them something really personal like that. It just doesn't fit into what I consider to be acceptable social behavior. I wouldn't walk up to somebody and say, "What do you do for a living?" I might say, "Hi, what's your name?" Anything I'd ask somebody is usually in an effort to get to know them better.

But they have no interest in me other than that they're curious and they can't place me. And I find that offensive. They say it like, "Oh, I like your T-shirt. Where did you get it?" They say it on that level, and I don't think people realize that it's a lot more personal than that. My ethnic background is a highly personal thing.

Plus it's a pain to explain. I usually just say, "My mother is white and my father is black." But in doing so, I don't feel like I've explained anything, and that frustrates me too, because my biological father is black, but the man who I consider to be my father is white. And that's what gets left out of the equation, and that bothers me. It's just such an oversimplification, and I know people don't want to know any of the intimate details.

There are times when I will just not answer people. They'll say, "Well, are you this?" and I'll say no. And I know very well that they are going to keep asking me until they get some sort of an answer. But I guess I'm trying to make the point that it really isn't their business. I don't like people just walking up to me out of the blue and asking me questions like that.

Many of the people I spoke to said being ambiguous-looking or hard to place was a positive thing. Some of them talked about turning the tables on the people who misidentify and mislabel them. They found ways to use their chameleon-like looks for their own advantage and amusement.

IT'S FUN BLOWING PEOPLE AWAY

ERIC KOJI STOWE, twenty-six
Sacramento, California
Mother: Japanese-American
Father: African-American

When I was growing up—it sounds kind of bad—I felt like I was a better person because I was a combination of two ethnicities. I felt stronger as a person, more dynamic as an individual. Like if you have just one chemical, that's one strength, and if you add another one, the combination is even stronger. My father told me that when I was a child, and I thought it was kind of cool.

I knew I was unique and looked different from all my friends. Everybody thought I was Filipino, or Mexican, or all African-American. But once they got a closer look, they could see that my eyes were the same as my mother's.

Once people found out that I was Japanese, or that I had learned the language, they kind of looked at me differently. That, plus the fact that I had an education—I blew away a lot of stereotypes. I worked at a Gap store. There were a lot of Japanese foreign students who would come in, and I would help them out. I'm six foot one and 190 pounds—and there would be this soft Japanese voice coming out. A lot of them were just speechless. It's fun blowing people away. That's my own little weapon, a little extra part of me.

25

YOU'RE SPECIAL

GENIA LINEAR, fourteen
Honolulu, Hawaii
Mother: Puerto Rican, Portuguese
Father: African-American, Native American

I like attention. If I'm walking around at a swap meet or something, people just stare at me and my sister, and they stare at my mom, 'cause my mom looks white. I guess they're trying to figure out what I am.

I was born in Hawaii. Practically everyone is biracial here. I'm Puerto Rican, black, Portuguese, Native American, Caucasian. There's this girl, she's pure Filipino, and she's like, "I wish I had all those races that you have." It's like a person with straight hair wants to have curly hair, and the person who has curly hair wants to have straight hair.

People would ask me, "Oh, what are you?" . . . "Oh, cool, cool." They think it's unique. I never heard anybody say, "You're half black, half white? Eww! What happened to you? What's wrong with your parents?"

I like it when people ask me what I am. You get to show your pride and stuff. I'm not saying that being pure is bad or anything. I just think that being mixed is like—you're special.

MY LOOK SAYS NOTHING ABOUT WHO I AM

MICHAEL LOGAN, twenty-three
Yuba City, California
Biological Mother: Thai
Stepmother: European-American (Scottish)
Father: European-American (Irish)

What I like most is that my look says nothing about who I am. There are stereotypes of Asians, blacks, whites, Hispanics, et cetera. When you look at me, you can't tell what I am. I think it's positive in the sense that, when somebody doesn't know what you are, they don't bring whatever prejudices they have into their interaction with you.

Also, what is it to be one person who's two things? People don't know what that is. They don't get any information about mixed-race people from the media, and chances are, they know few others.

People don't readily dismiss me based on their own stereotypes, because I don't fit within the framework of their knowledge. They don't say, "He is Asian, and here is what I know about Asians, and so here is how I must interact with him." So they want to find out, "Who is this person?" And that means they get past the looks to find out about me. They have to put in a little bit more work to get to know who I am.

27

I GOT TO SEE HIS TRUE COLORS

BRIAN HARRIS, sixteen
Stanton, California
Mother: European-American
Father: African-American

Most people can't tell that I'm mixed. It's kind of weird, because, since I don't look like I'm part black, people will say things they wouldn't say if they knew that I *was*. Like when I was in seventh grade, there was this kid in my history class and he sat in front of me and he was kind of like my friend. One day the teacher said the school was going to be sending home report cards. He raised his hand and he said, "Well, my report card is not going to get to my house. My dog attacks the mailman."

And then the teacher was like, "Why does your dog attack the mailman?"

He said, "Because the mailman is black."

The teacher said, "Well, then maybe you'll have to pick it up at the office."

He turned around and he said, "I'm proud of my dog. I taught it to attack those . . ." and he didn't say "those black people," he used some very derogatory words. Then he made sure he said, "But I didn't teach it to attack Mexican people," because he was assuming that I was Mexican, so he thought that I would be fine with that.

And I said, "Do you know that my dad's black?"

He said, "Oh, yeah, yeah, right," laughing at me, thinking I was trying to scare him or something.

A girl heard me say that and she said, "His dad *is* black."

He went from laughing to being serious, and then he was like, "I was just joking. My best friend is black. I like black people."

I was like, you've already shown your true colors.

I realized that he was an ignorant person, and I knew that he wasn't someone I wanted to hang around with. So it was a good thing that he couldn't tell what race I was, because I learned something about him that I wouldn't have learned otherwise.

THEY LIKE VERY DIFFERENT-LOOKING MODELS

ALEXANDRA WINNER

NIKKOLE PALMATIER, twenty-two
Okemos, Michigan
Mother: Japanese
Father: European-American

My mom is from Hokkaido. It's in northern Japan. My dad was in the army and he was stationed there. He taught English too. My mom's younger sister was one of his students. She introduced **29** them and they started dating. They had a Japanese wedding in Japan. The pictures are just incredible, because my dad's six foot six inches tall and my mom's five foot two. So it's like all these short little Japanese people and then this big tall white guy. My mom had a beautiful traditional silk kimono. My dad wore the traditional men's kimono.

My mom is the only one of her family who's here in the States. So we try to go back to Japan every four or five years. I remember when I was sixteen, me and my dad and my mom were walking in Yokohama, which is a relatively big city, and this little kid and his mom stopped my dad. She asked if he would take a picture with her son because he was so much taller than her little boy and she thought it was a cool contrast. I just remember going, "Why are people stopping us to take pictures?" We really stuck out like crazy. We were like a big circus show.

I'm almost five foot ten inches tall. When I was sixteen, I went to Tokyo to try to model. I visited with the Elite modeling agency in Tokyo, and they just said, "Hmm, you're not quite what we're looking for." They had a problem with me because my lips are full and my hair is really curly.

A lot of the celebrities there are mixed, half Japanese. Most of them have a lot of Caucasian features, but they still look very Asian, whereas I just don't look Asian. If I pull my hair completely back and if my makeup is done a certain way, you can see maybe a hint of it. I remember when I was eight years old and we went to Japan, my mom would put my hair in braids or make me wear it up.

Most people think I'm Hispanic. When my boyfriend met me, he thought I was Middle Eastern. I model here in Chicago, and my agent markets me as Hispanic or black. I don't even get called for a lot of Asian jobs. I've done catalogue work for Sears, Montgomery Ward, and Spiegel, mostly here in Chicago. I used to do a lot of runway work because they like very different-looking models. I'm listed under "ethnic models."

How I look is an advantage, definitely. I get sent out for a lot of jobs. They don't just send me out on the Asian calls. They'll submit my picture for black things too. I actually did the '94 and '95 *Ebony* Fashion Fair Tour. It's sponsored by *Ebony* magazine. I was on the road for seven months. We toured around the United States and went to 185 different cities. I was one of twelve girls picked. I think I was one of the first Asian models to ever do that.

WHATEVER YOU THINK I AM IS FINE

GARY MURAOKA, twenty-three
Gilroy, California
Mother: European-American (French, Irish, Welsh, German)
Father: Japanese-American

I grew up in a predominantly Hispanic community. It's a small community. The demographics here are 60 percent Hispanic, 5 percent Asian, 8 percent black, and the rest Caucasian.

I guess everybody thought I was Hispanic because all of my friends were Hispanic. I just blended in with them like a chameleon. I didn't make an issue out of it. I was like, "Yeah, whatever you think I am is fine."

Some people may take offense at the idea of a half-Japanese person playing it off to be a Chicano, but in high school, it worked and made my life easier. I tell people the truth. If they ask, I go, "I'm half Oriental." But then they look at me sort of funny. Even full-blooded Japanese do not believe me. They think **31** it's weird that I might know a little Japanese when I order lunch at a Japanese restaurant.

I was working on patrol one day. I was assisting an officer to book a combative drunk who felt that the police were picking on him just because he was Mexican and the arresting officer was white. He looked at me and said, "You're Chicano—you know what I'm talking about." His blood alcohol level was at least .25 and he couldn't even stand up on his own two feet. I agreed with him and assured him that everything was going according to the law.

For him to identify with someone who he believed was the same race calmed him way down. Even though I had to mislead him about my race, it prevented the use of force, and we were able to do our job effectively and peacefully.

The next three people had the strongest feelings about the way others often perceive their physical appearance.

I DON'T LIKE PEOPLE MAKING ASSUMPTIONS ABOUT ME

JENNIFER HO, twenty-four
Oakland, California
Mother: European-American (English, French, Irish, Scottish)
Father: Chinese-American

When I was growing up, there was always the question, "What are you?" Or, "Are you something? You look kind of exotic." I still get these questions all the time, but I also think a lot of people assume I'm white.

It would have been very easy for me to "pass" as white and just have all white friends. Most of the people I came into contact with—in terms of my education and social activities—were white. In so many ways I could have just locked myself into that and been white. But I didn't let that happen.

It was always very important for me to have friends who weren't white in addition to friends who were. And I didn't really understand that at the time. I didn't even do it consciously. I had so many friends who were not only minorities but who also had parents from foreign countries. They came from a different culture and yet were adapting to American life, and somehow I just found it easier to relate to people like that. Looking back on my choices in life and the choices I made about friends, I just know that those were the people who I related to best.

I never encountered outright prejudice from people, but I always knew that there was something different about me. There were just these comments here and there. There were things I experienced and knew about that they just didn't.

I remember when I was ten and I had this friend and we were in this Chinese restaurant. She'd come with me and my parents, and we were having dinner. And she said in a really loud voice, "I think it's so sad that Chinese people don't have eyelashes."

I remember thinking, "What? How can you say that? I have eyelashes. My dad has eyelashes." But she hadn't ever looked closely enough. She hadn't been around Chinese or Asian people enough to realize that they have eyelashes—they may be small, but they're there. She also didn't realize she was talking to Chinese people—she didn't think of me that way, and I guess she thought that my dad had been whitewashed by marrying my mom. **33**

When I went to college, I would meet people and hang out with them for long periods of time and a lot of them wouldn't know that I was Asian. And when they found out, they would say, "Oh, this totally changes the way I think about you and you're so much cooler and more interesting now."

That was a shock. Why would finding out that I was part Asian change the way they thought about me? And why was I more interesting and cooler now? To have people just automatically make the assumption that I was white, and to keep it for months and months after I had known them, was really disturbing to me. It's important for me to have people recognize what I am because that's very much a part of who I am, and I don't like people making assumptions about me.

Another reason it bothers me is because of some of the reactions I've had from people who have assumed that I'm white. I'd say, "No, I'm not white."

And they'd be like, "You're not? But you are."

These are white people and they would say stuff to me like, "Why are you making such a big deal about it? Why do you care? You look white, so you are white." I've even had people say that I'm lucky that I can pass for white—that I should be grateful. I can sense that they're annoyed that I make a point over it, that I am stubborn about saying, "Don't call me white, because I'm not." I think that it makes those people really uncomfortable and I think that they would just prefer that I let them think that I'm white. And that pisses me off a lot.

It also makes me angry because they're very condescending about it. It's like, "Shut up and pass for white," as if it's a gift that they do this for me, like a privilege I have. That's really offensive to me.

Other minorities—especially Hispanics and blacks—notice it much more. They may not know what I am, but they'll ask me about it. They're just more sensitive to that kind of stuff, I guess. They look for it because it is more of an issue in their lives than it is in most white people's lives. I guess that's what annoys me most—people don't look closely enough.

It's important for me to be recognized as what I am—not white, not Asian, because I really don't feel like I'm either of those things. I'm mixed, which is something completely unique.

WHY ARE PEOPLE STARING AT ME?

NICOLE RIVERA, seventeen
Bay Shore, New York
Mother: African-American
Father: Puerto Rican

When I was in second grade, this little boy—he was Argentinian—invited me to his birthday party. I went and I had fun, and my mom came to pick me up. Well, the next day in school he goes, "I would have never invited you to my birthday party if I had known you were black." And I punched him.

I couldn't imagine that coming out of somebody's mouth who is that small. His parents must have said something.

35

I don't have the same skin color as my mother—she has darker skin. When I go to the store with her, the salesperson will go, "Are you together?" Or, "Next."

My dad is light-skinned. So my friends always ask me, "Is your dad white?"

My hair throws people off too. People are always looking at my hair trying to figure out what the hell I am. I have really thick black hair. I use black hair products and I only go to black hairdressers. People are always like, "Wait a minute. She's light-skinned, but look at her hair!"

I get mad because people are always trying to categorize me. People try to figure me out like I'm some puzzle. That's really annoying. I can understand that people are curious, but they ask me questions all the time. Why can't they leave me alone? I am what I am. I really respect the people who get to know me first and ask me later.

But the people who come up to me and say, "What are you?"— I have no clue why they want to know. There's a group of black girls at my high school, and they'll always make snide comments to me. They'll go, "What are you? Are you white and black? Are you Indian?" Just the way they ask is obnoxious too. It's kind of like, "What are you—you alien?" They're poking and probing.

Sometimes they're like, "Look at that black girl trying to act white." Or, "Look at that Puerto Rican girl trying to act black." My boyfriend is black, and sometimes when I walk down the hall with him, they say, "Why is he going out with that white girl?" Or, "Why is he going out with that Puerto Rican girl?" Maybe he's going out with me because he likes me. You learn to brush it off, because people are just ignorant.

Ignorance is fear of the unknown. If you're ignorant about something, then you're scared of it. Well, I'm not scared of Latino people and I'm not scared of black people. I feel lucky to know both sides. I'm a more open-minded individual because of that. I have friends who are white, and I have friends who are Puerto Rican, friends from Colombia, friends who are black.

I'm lucky because I have two cultures instead of just one. My dad never taught me Spanish, but I hang out with my friends who are Puerto Rican and I pick up things from them. And I listen to salsa and merengue. And I listen to R&B and rap. I eat Hispanic food and I listen to the Spanish radio station.

But at the same time, being both has kind of made me self-conscious. People see me in so many different ways. So I'm never sure if people are treating me a certain way because of what I look like or because of who I am. Something will happen and I'll be like, "Is this a racial thing? Or is it just because they don't like me?"

I'll say to my boyfriend, "Why are people staring at me, trying to figure out what I am?"

He'll say, "How do you know they're not just saying, 'Oh, wow, that's a nice shirt,' or 'I like her hair'?" Sometimes I think he's right. But I feel like I'm not understood sometimes. He's trying to understand, but you can't understand it unless you've experienced it.

People are ignorant, you know. Maybe eventually they'll learn—when everyone is the same shade of gray.

I'M JUST AN OBJECT TO PEOPLE

JENNIFER CHAU, twenty
Queens, New York
Mother: Jewish European-American
Father: Chinese-American

All of my experience as a biracial woman has been based on appearance. People will ask me what I am before they ask me what my name is.

When I first meet someone, we'll be talking and they'll be staring at my face and not really listening to what I'm saying. And then, finally, "So, what are you?" That question always pops up. It disturbs me when people are more interested in that than in what I'm saying or what I'm thinking.

And people always have this assumption that all biracial people are beautiful and that that's the best thing about us. People say, "Oh, I wish I was biracial because biracial people are the most beautiful people." Biracial people are just really objectified, you know?

I see that happening constantly to my biracial friends—just so much focus on the physical. You're just a shell, there's nothing inside. People don't try to find out what's inside, they're just concerned with the outside, because it's so mystical and mysterious.

It's frustrating to think of so many people looking at you, and that's all you are to them—just something to look at. It's very dehumanizing. I'm just an object to people, I'm not a person. I have no feelings. I have no thoughts. I'm just an object, basically. That's how many people make me feel.

THE COLOR OF MY SKIN IS NOT THE COLOR OF MY HEART

TYONEK GLEE OGEMAGESHIG, twenty-four
Taholah, Washington
Mother: European-American, Mexican
Father: Native American

I've been on the Quinault Indian Reservation since I was in eighth grade. It's on the Olympic Peninsula in the northwest part of Washington State. Before that, we lived on Flathead Indian Reservation in western Montana. I've actually lived all my life on reservations. It's a different mentality than living in a city or living in a white community. That Indian thing is always there, the Indian beliefs.

My mom is half white and half Mexican. My dad's family was originally from White Earth Reservation, a small reservation in north-central Minnesota. They're enrolled members of the Pembina band of the Minnesota Chippewa tribe.

My dad had a really hard time when he was a kid. My grandma had to struggle to keep her family together because she and my grandfather went their separate ways. My dad experienced a lot of racism, and he told me stories. He went to a high school that had a lot of white people in it. A couple of the guys would gang up on him and this other Indian. They'd try and beat them up just because they were Indians. He fought back and kicked their asses. Whatever he has against white people was put into concrete then. Now he has a hard time being around people who aren't Indian.

He's in court right now for discrimination against him by his employer. When you work your whole life and people treat you like dirt, it's hard to feel comfortable in the outer world. I have a lot of respect for what he's had to endure. I try to follow his example—stand tall, chin up. He's like a modern Indian warrior.

I may be part Mexican and part white and part Indian, but in my heart I see myself as just Indian. Being mixed has been a pretty big issue in my life—trying to figure out who I am as a person. I'm probably the lightest person in my family. When I was younger, I'd say, "I don't look Indian, so I guess I'm not." When I was growing up, I'd look at my sister and she'd be so much darker than I was, so I'd think, "Who am I?" I'd look at my dad and he would look real dark—if he gets out in the sun he tans easily. And my mom's darker than I am. But I have a hard time even getting a tan.

To me, being Indian is about knowing the culture. But in so many ways, it's just how you look at a quick glance. Someone can't look at me and be able to tell I'm Indian. So I have to tell people. At this time in my life I practically shout it at people.

If you're dark or you can get dark, you don't really have to deal with that—that physicality of not being able to look like who you are. Like when my sister is among Indians she can be accepted just like that. You'd never have to ask her—everyone knows she is an Indian. It's obvious. But I have to work at it a little bit, make an extra effort to get to know them. Indians would be like, "Oh, you're her brother?" I was Indian because I was her brother, not because I was me.

In a way, they don't really accept that I am Indian. They keep me at a distance until I do something that proves that I am, and sometimes I feel like I shouldn't have to do that. What ends up happening is that my worldview comes out in my actions. After they talk to me for a couple of minutes, they can tell I'm Indian because the culture in me comes out—how I feel and how I think and how I see the world.

Because my sister's so much darker than I am, she's encountered racist remarks and stuff. I can be right next to her and they're not even directed at me. Once we were on a school bus and these two guys gave my sister a dirty look and said something to each other. So I said, "What are you looking at? Leave her alone." To them, she was just an Indian. A drunk, a bitch, a whore—that's all they saw in her. All they knew were labels and stereotypes, not her.

In high school, Indians didn't get along with white people. Just before this [incident on the bus] happened, there had been this huge fight. There was a party at the beach and these Indians showed up. People were talking about it all over school because a lot of real popular white guys got beat up. Those guys on the bus just projected their feelings and stereotypes about Indians on my sister.

My sister can handle her own stuff—she's a pretty tough cookie. But those views or opinions weren't voiced at me, they were voiced at her, and that made me so mad. I felt like I wasn't really Indian enough if somebody didn't act racist toward me. I was kind of ashamed that I didn't look more like my sister. And I was ashamed that I didn't look more like how I felt inside.

It was a hard thing to deal with, and my dad used to talk to me a lot about it. He would always sit me down and get to the core of what I was feeling and help me try to get over it. He said, "You should feel lucky because you can walk in two worlds. That's not a problem, it's a gift and it's a strength. In the long run, it's going to be a power. You will be able to do things that I would never be able to." He told me this many times. I'd feel proud for a while and then I'd feel ashamed again.

I had a hard time making friends at the reservation. I got bused to a high school, and most of the people there were white. I had a hard time relating to them too. It seemed like I didn't fit in anywhere. I worked hard in school and I didn't slack off and I was kind of a nerd, I guess. But I think that a major cause of the anxiety and stress of socializing was that I was mixed and didn't seem to fit in with either group. It made me less friendly. I think if I were darker it would have been easier to fit in.

But when I got to be seventeen, things changed. What my dad told me finally made sense. And ever since then, opening doors, or trying to prove myself, or doing all this extra stuff to be accepted doesn't bother me anymore. I finally realized that that's just a part of life. I think people relate to other people better if they appear to be the same. If you look the same, they'll feel more comfortable about letting you into their world.

I don't get scared and I don't get annoyed because I have to do a little bit of extra work. I think it makes me a stronger person. I believe that the harder you work at something the better you become. I think a person who is mixed always has to work harder to come to terms with who he or she is than somebody who is Indian or somebody who is white. I think that what I had to go through was bad, but it helped me understand who I am.

I asked my dad if I could take my grandfather's name. My name used to be Johnson and I changed it to Ogemageshig. Johnson is a white name. If people call you Ty Johnson, they don't know you're Indian. But if your name is Ogemageshig, there's no doubt. So people are always like, "What kind of name is that?"

I always have to tell them, "This is how you say it, this is what it means, this is what nationality this is." Now my name kind of opens doors for me. I thank my grandfather for that. Changing my name was a way of finally taking that stand. It was kind of a representation of how I felt and who I wanted to be.

Before, I was ashamed and I didn't understand who I was. It's kind of the opposite now—instead of being ashamed I'm proud of everything I am. I'm loud and vocal about Indians and Red Power. You've gotta be loud and tell people who you are.

At the Quinault Indian Reservation, a lot of people look up to me because I'm going to school out east. I'm kind of a role model. There are a lot of people I don't even know who keep track of how I'm doing.

There were so many bad things I saw when I was growing up—the poverty, the alcohol and drug problems—things that I want to help improve and make better on the reservations. I knew that to help fix those problems I had to get an education and come back and work. That gave me my motivation to strive and work hard in my classes. I want to go to law school or maybe teach.

By my actions—by dedicating my life to school and trying to succeed and work for Indian people—I have made them see that the color of my skin is not the color of my heart. I don't have to prove myself anymore.

CHECK ONE BOX

Race. Check one.

❏ White
❏ Asian/Pacific Islander
❏ Hispanic
❏ American Indian/Alaskan Native
❏ Black

If you've taken a standardized test or applied for college, you've had to answer a question like this. It implies that race is a natural and important way to categorize people. And it states that there are a few distinct or "pure" racial groups—five in this case—and that each of us can be pigeonholed into one of them.

Although there are obviously differences in skin color and other physical features among people, do these differences justify dividing humanity into color-coded types—red, yellow, black, white, and brown? Absolutely not, say a growing chorus of scientists and other luminaries. The anthropologist Mark Nathan Cohen, author of Culture of Intolerance: Chauvinism, Class, and Racism in the United States *(Yale University Press, 1998), has much to say about this: "Dividing people up by color is like dividing cars up by color. Color is a superficial add-on. The same is true of skin color in people."*

Scientists estimate that only a measly 6 to 10 genes out of the 30,000 to 40,000 genes that make up a human being are responsible for skin color. "The number of genes devoted to your skin color are trivial. It's something like .01 percent," Cohen continues. And knowing someone's skin color doesn't tell you much about the other 99.99 percent of his or her DNA. "You can't tell who is biologically more similar to whom in a crowded room by looking at color." You may well share more genes or DNA with a person of a different race than with somebody of your own race. The lives of many people have been saved by a blood transfusion from someone of another race, while receiving blood from someone of the same race but an incompatible blood type would have killed them.

Skin pigment, like other physical traits, is simply an adaptation to the environment—climate, diet, and other factors. For example, dark skin is an adaptation to strong ultraviolet light around the equator. "There are dark-skinned populations all around the equator. But those people aren't related to each other. Blackness is not a sign of ancient relationships." Scientists have found that dark-skinned Africans are more genetically similar to Europeans than they are to equally dark-pigmented Australian aborigines.

Skin color is a trait that varies so much within "racial" groups that it's meaningless anyway, adds Jonathan Marks, a biological anthropologist at the University of California at Berkeley, who wrote about race in his book Human Biodiversity *(Aldine de Gruyter, 1995). Professors Marks and Cohen and many of their colleagues use words such as "race," "mixed-race," "black," and "white" with quote marks around them because they feel so strongly that these terms are misleading. "The problem," says Marks, "is that 'white' people range from pale Norwegians to swarthy Italians; and even very dark-skinned people often fall into the category 'white' because they facially resemble Europeans, yet are [more darkly] pigmented (for example, Pakistanis). Likewise 'black' ranges from the skin tones of Lena Horne to Wesley Snipes."*

Not all dark-skinned people have full lips. Similarly, not all light-skinned people have narrow noses, and not all Asians have almond-shaped eyes. Notes Cohen: "I've got pictures of people from East Africa who are very dark and yet have very narrow noses, much narrower than do most Europeans. I've got pictures of Australian aboriginals who are dark-skinned and have wavy or straight hair with blond or red highlights. I can easily find you white people with noses as broad as or broader than those of most **47**

Africans. I've shown my classes pictures of people who are Chinese, and my students don't believe it because they look Caucasian."

Scientists have yet to find a single biological trait that all white people share or a gene that all Asians carry. There are no biological traits that mark all members of a particular race.

" 'Race' is a powerful optical illusion. 'Race' is not biologically real," says Professor Marks. It's culturally real. "It's a way in which we confer identity upon ourselves. Depending on which traits you look at, you can draw boundaries around groups of people in many different ways, all of which are biological to a certain extent, but none of which are objective." The decisions about where to draw lines dividing people are made on the basis of economic, social, and political considerations—and not science.

For example, says Marks, we draw a line separating the peoples of Africa from the peoples of Europe and Asia. But Africans are actually quite a diverse group, as are both Asians and Europeans. "Any way you look at them—genetically, physically, physiologically—the Somali in East Africa and the Iraqi in West Asia are going to be more similar to each other than the Somali is to a Nigerian or the Iraqi is to a Swede." Yet, since the late 1600s, the enormous differences among African peoples have been downplayed in the West, while the differences between Africans and Europeans have been emphasized. "What you have going on in the 1600s is colonialism and the slave trade. In Europe, it became expedient to view all Africans as the same."

Interbreeding is what accounts for the amazing similarities among human beings and the fact that so-called pure races don't exist. There have always been trade networks and wars that have brought people from different parts of the world together. And wherever people have come into contact with each other, there has been intermixing.

48

In the United States, there has been extensive racial mixing for centuries. Many African-Americans—estimates are at 30 percent or more—are said to have some Native American or European-American ancestry. People who are identified as Hispanics or Latinos in the United States are by and large racially mixed. And many Native Americans, as well as whites, have mixed ancestry. For example, genetic testing recently revealed that Thomas Jefferson's family includes descendants of the offspring of Jefferson and his multiracial slave Sally Hemings.

As the numbers of people who claim their mixed-race heritage increase, it will be harder for Americans to cling to the belief that race and racial categories make any sense.

I'VE NEVER FIT INTO ANY CATEGORY

AMANDA HOLZHAUER, sixteen
Cleveland Heights, Ohio
Mother: African-American
Father: European-American (German, Swiss)

I was in the chemistry room one day putting my books down and two African-American girls walked in. They were talking about interracial marriage—how they wouldn't support the idea; they **49** wouldn't want anyone in their family to get into an interracial marriage.

I got up and followed them down the hallway listening to their discussion and I said, "You know what? I really don't have a problem with interracial marriage, because if my parents did I wouldn't be here."

And they turned and looked at me and one of them said, "Oh, my God, Amanda, I forgot you were mixed. But that's okay, because you're not really white—you're black."

I'm like, "Hmm, okay." And then I mentioned the name of another mixed girl at the school and I said, "What do you consider her?"

And they said, "Oh, she's white."

I don't know how they make these distinctions. Maybe it's the way you act. Or maybe it's just the way they want to think of you—if they like you, you're what they are; if they don't, you're what they're not.

Like if someone's mad at me, they'll give me a derogatory name based on the part of me that's not like them. I was hanging out with some African-American kids and one of them got mad at me and said, "You white whore." Instead of just saying "whore" she decided to say "white whore." If I'm hanging out with white people, they sometimes call me a "black bitch." They go back and forth depending on whether they like you or not.

One instance sticks in my mind. For Catholic Schools Week we had a door-decorating contest at my school. So, after school, some of us were working on the classroom door. An African-American boy walked in and he said, "So, Amanda, what do you consider yourself?"

"I'm an American."

"No, no—I mean black or white?"

"I'm an American."

"No, which one? One or the other."

"You're obviously not getting the point." And one of the African-American girls who walked in with him told him to shut up because he had no clue what he was talking about. He gave her a nasty look and walked out of the room. I was upset that he had to be so blind. But it made me feel good that the girl seemed to catch on to the idea.

It's so incredibly annoying that people can't get past racial lines. When it happens, I think, "Great, here's another one of those people who is not going to be able to understand anything about me."

People tend to want to label me one or the other. To make me say I'm one or the other is like making me deny one of my parents and a part of myself. It's like making me deny what I am, because I'm not white and I'm not black—I'm both. My parents raised me to be proud of both cultures. My dad used to talk about his German blood, he's always proud of that. And my mom is proud of her African-American heritage. And my dad tries to make me appreciate my African-American culture, and my mom, my German culture.

I try not to let what other people think of me define me. I refuse to limit myself in the way they want me to.

People feel safe when there are definite little borderlines. People like to find common links with other people and cling to them. It makes them feel safe to feel similar so they don't have to worry about being alone. But I've never fit into any category that people have tried to shove me into. There should be no groups, in my mind. Just get rid of them.

I AM NOT AN OTHER

CANDACE REA, nineteen
Kaneohe, Hawaii
Mother: European-American
Father: Filipino-American

One thing that has come to bother me more and more in recent years is how to classify myself ethnically or racially on applications and surveys. I have trouble deciding whether to check the "white" box or the "Asian" box, because I don't want to deny either side of my heritage.

But I have even more of a conflict when I check the box marked "other." I am not an other and have never been an other. I am a person of mixed race. I don't belong in some outcast category. I am a person just like everyone else.

I would like to be recognized for the racially mixed person I am. So far, I have only had the chance to check a box marked "biracial" once in my life.

While I was working on this book, a controversy was raging over whether or not the federal government should change the way it categorizes race and, if so, how. Several options were being considered. One option was the creation of a separate stand-alone multiracial box. A more popular option combined a new multira-

cial category with a list of races that a person would check off. These ideas eventually lost out to another choice, "check one or more" boxes or races.

At first, Monina Diaz was in favor of the multiracial box option. She was excited about the possibility of having her own box— a multiracial box—on the census and other federal forms. However, she later changed her mind. In explaining why, Monina analyzes the role of race in the United States and describes the ways in which multiracial people are forced to deny who they are in order to fit in.

RACE DOESN'T EXIST

MONINA DIAZ, twenty
Monrovia, California
Mother: African-American
Father: Puerto Rican

Princeton requires you to do independent work each semester. My major is in the Woodrow Wilson School; it's public policy and international affairs. They put you into a task force with other students. I chose the task force dealing with revising directive 15 for the census 2000. My topic is to research a multiracial category for the census—the pros and cons of that and whether that's the best thing for multiracial individuals.

53

I'm the only person who perceives herself as multiracial in the class. Some of my task force members say, "I don't see the problem—check a box, and be through." And it's very disturbing that people feel that way. There was one guy in my school who said, "What a useless task force. What's the point?" There's a huge point to it. But talking to people and hearing their viewpoints showed me that some people just don't understand.

When I first started the class I was like—hands down— multiracial category, no question. I've had so many issues all my life, issues about not having a community, and I would like a category. I felt like the multiracial category would give me a community. People need groups.

But now I would be in favor of checking all boxes that apply. I think the worst thing to do would be to put a multiracial category in the census, because, in effect, you would be buying into the system—a system that you've detested all your life, a system that pressures you to fit into some group. So now you have a group, and now you fit into it, but what does that do for racial problems in America? I would hate to see the creation of more racial divisions.

I guess the most striking thing about my research is that I've come to the realization that race does not exist—it's a social construct. These racial categories were constructed totally for economic, political, and social reasons; they're not based on anything, especially anything scientific or biological. It's almost impossible to put people into these categories.

I think race is so entrenched and so ingrained in American thought and the way we view people that it's hard to see that. For example, whether they admit it or not, most people who consider themselves all black aren't really all black. And Hispanics who consider themselves truly Latino aren't really all Latino. I mean, what does Latino mean? It's being Indian, black, and white/Spanish. Most blacks are a mixture of the same components: African, white, and Indian. If you look at black people, it's almost hideous to put them into one group, because you have some people who are so light and they're still considered black because of "the rules of hypodescent."* And then you have some people who are very dark who are considered black—there's just that big range.

You have the exact opposite rule for Native Americans. Whereas for blacks, one drop of "black blood" makes you black, for Native Americans you almost have to prove that you have enough Indian blood—at least a quarter, or whatever—to be considered Native American. It's political, because the dominant group, which maintains complete political and economic power—in this case, white people—didn't want to give more money or land to Indians, but they wanted to have as many slaves as they possibly could. And that still affects the way people think.

I especially see it at Princeton because it's very socially segregated. You have all these different people and they align themselves along these socially constructed lines. You put them into a dorm, they align themselves. You put them into a cafeteria, they align themselves. You put them into a class, they align themselves. You put them into a group of three people in a class—I've seen this in my French class—and it'll be like the two white people and the one black person. And it's because they perceive themselves as different, even though race doesn't exist. I think that none of these racial problems that we have are ever going to

---

*The American belief, which was at times formalized by law, that a mixed-race person belongs in one of the groups that make up his or her heritage—the lowest status group. This is also called the "one-drop rule," and has been applied most often to people with African ancestry. For example, someone who has a black parent and a white parent would be considered black, not multiracial or white.

go away as long as people keep seeing other people as the "other," or the people they don't identify with.

I don't know what it's like not to live in a house where there are different ethnicities, different cultures. It's very normal for me to have Spanish rice and fried chicken and greens for dinner. I've never known anything else. And my brothers and sisters all look completely different as far as color, and that's normal to me. We have had different experiences, but I think for all of us, being multiracial has been an issue. It's only been a hurtful issue when we step out of our house.

When I was at school, I just knew that I was different. First of all, I never felt completely accepted by either group—blacks or Hispanics. My hair was different. My features were kind of different. I was definitely black, but I wasn't black enough for black people. Hispanics knew my last name was Hispanic and knew I was Hispanic, but I was never Hispanic enough. I remember times when I wished I was just all black or just all Puerto Rican, but that would be such an affront to one of my parents. I think that goes with the pressure to fit into a category.

In school, I remember some people who accepted both sides of me, but that was very rare. There's pressure from both sides to almost forsake your other side. My black and Latino friends acknowledged and knew that I'm Puerto Rican and black or black and Puerto Rican, but while I was with them I couldn't be both at the same time. I had to affirm the culture they belonged to. So when I was with my black friends, I couldn't be Monina who's black and Puerto Rican, I had to be Monina who's black. Then when I was with my Latino friends, I had to very much assert my Latina-ness.

Around black people, black girls particularly, I didn't talk about my Puerto Rican–ness at all. I didn't talk about my Latina-ness because I knew I would experience bad repercussions for asserting anything other than black. It's always seen as "You think you're better than us" or "You want to be white and you don't want to be like us and have our status."

If someone asked me, I would say, "My dad's Latino, my mom's black." Otherwise I'd just let them think what they wanted. To some extent, that's probably how I kept my friends who happened to be black. I know for a fact that if I had been outspoken about my mixed-ness and said, "Well, you know I'm black and Puerto Rican," and really claimed that in front of them, I would have had a very different experience. I wouldn't have been as well liked, I would've been bashed, I'm sure. Around them I was black, around my Hispanic friends I was Puerto Rican, and that was that. I was always divided and separated to them.

In high school, I met another Blatina [a combination of black and Latina] girl. Her mom is Mexican and her dad's black. We were very close friends, and that was really good for me because finally there was someone who completely understood. When I was with her, it was totally okay to be these two things.

But even though we were together, it was still an issue that there wasn't a community for us. There was no black-Hispanic community. But we had to go somewhere. So we were still aligning ourselves one way or the other. I remember we went through our phases together. At one point we were just completely black. We did "black culture." We dressed black and we listened to black music, and it wasn't wrong because that is part of our culture. But we kind of de-emphasized our Hispanic side.

Then there was the other time, when we dressed Hispanic and we went to Hispanic parties and we got into the whole Hispanic thing. We fiercely celebrated Cinco de Mayo and the whole bit.

I think it [trying on different cultures] was really healthy. I know some multiracial individuals here and I see them doing sim- **57** ilar things. And I think it's probably something that you have to do. And I think that it made me a lot stronger.

I'm from L.A. and the Latino community is becoming a majority in the state, if we are not already. I'm afraid that there will be a time when you'll have to pick your affiliations and where you stand. Are you this or are you that? Are you with us or are you against us? You'll have to draw your lines and that would be a horrible thing to have to do.

"BLACK DOMINATES"

Maria (second from right) with her parents, Doug and Pat; sister, Gina; and four half-brothers, Gary, Douglas Jr., Emmanuel, and Paul.

MARIA BARNER, twenty-one
Norfolk, Virginia
Mother: European-American
Father: African-American

When I was in fifth grade I had a teacher and I hated her so much. She was always mean. We had one of those tests and I had to fill out my racial category. I think I put "other." I just put something different—other than "black." And she really went off. She was like, "Why did you do this?"

I said, " 'Cause my mom's white and my dad's black."

She said, "Change this to black. You're black because your father's black, and you have his last name so you're automatically black. So just forget the white side." She said that black dominates. She was black.

I was very emotional back then. I went home crying and told my mom. She raised hell when she got to the school and the teacher got a slap on the wrist. I stayed in her class. But needless to say, she didn't like me for the rest of the year.

I think that biracial people might be more accepted by black people than by white people around here, 'cause if you have a little bit of black in you you're automatically a minority. I don't think I'll ever pass for being white but I can kind of pass for being black. When white people look at me, they see black. But black people look at me and say, "Well, you might be black, but you've got to be something else." They always say Puerto Rican. I haven't really had a white person say I'm Puerto Rican; they just see black features so they just put me in that group.

I'm black and white but I've almost always put black when I had to write something down. I didn't want to put "other," because it is considered Asian or something. I figured that since most of my friends were black, and I had most of those traits, and I was more accepted by black people, I would just put black. In high school and college I started putting black and white, or I would alternate between them.

When I was in the ninth grade, I was taking a science exam— a national exam—and I had to fill out my racial category. I decided to have some fun this time, so I put black and then I filled in white too. The next day the teacher came up to me and said that there had been a problem with the test. The computer kept saying something was wrong. She noticed that I had marked two races and the computer was rejecting that.

She said, "You messed up the test. I had to go through them by hand and check everybody. So next time just pick one. If you want to pick black, put black—or put white—it doesn't matter, **59** just don't put both." It was like I had messed up her whole night or something.

My mom is involved with this Interracial Connections group and she told the group about it and that stirred up a lot of stuff. The leader of the group told the news people, so the news people came to my school to interview me and it was on television. And this was all just because I marked two things on the paper.

Since Maria had these experiences, the Norfolk Public School District has added a multiracial category as an option in questions about race.

I KNOW WHAT I AM

BRIAN HARRIS, sixteen
Stanton, California
Mother: European-American
Father: African-American

When he was twelve, Brian started an international pen pal service called Friendship Sees No Color. He pairs up each person with a pen pal of a different race. His pen pal service has had up to 20,000 members. He won a Prudential Spirit of America Award in 1997 for his hard work to educate people and reduce ignorance and intolerance.

When I was younger, I'd see talk shows on TV about someone who didn't like the fact that their white daughter was dating a black man. Invariably there was always someone who would stand up in the audience and say [to the couple], "Don't you realize what you are doing? You're going to have kids and they're going to be ruined," and stuff like that.

And I would always wish that they had someone on those shows who's biracial who would say, "Hey, that's not always true."

So I started writing to the shows and saying, "Just because you're biracial doesn't mean that you're destined to be ruined, that you're never going to have a normal life, that your parents did a terrible thing, and that you're never going to fit in." I wanted to go on those shows and say those things and tell people, "Hey, I'm biracial and I've never had any more problems than anybody else."

Once I got Friendship Sees No Color started, I started getting invited to these shows. The audiences are usually pretty nice. But then I went on *Judge for Yourself.* The show was called "Are White Women Stealing Black Men?" There was a black woman on who was really angry with white women who were marrying black men. She said that all the black men were being taken away. Then when the host asked me what race I called myself, she said, "He knows what race he is—he's black."

I said, "Well, no, I consider myself biracial."

And she said, "And so you're black."

I said, "What makes my black side more important than my white side? What makes my dad's side more important than my mom's?"

Then a man stood up and said that black is the dominant gene so I was black. I ended up arguing with these people. Usually, I'm pretty calm. But that time, I ended up turning red and yelling at people.

I've had people tell me that before—you know, "Regardless of what you think you are, you're black." But it's not going to affect **61** me because it's my personal choice what I want to call myself. So they can hate it, they can go to sleep at night crying about it—but it's not going to affect my choice. I mean, I know what I am.

HALF-BREED

I'm sometimes told that I don't fit in,
Told that I'll soon have troubles within.
I'm told to pick either black or white,
I think it over every night.
Should I give in and do as they say?
Or should I stay strong and have it my way?
Race is something you can't pick or choose,
Because if you do you will surely lose.
I know who I am and say it with pride,
As both black and white I experience the best of both sides.
I stand here proud of who I am,
Even if ignored by great Uncle Sam.
All I ask for is two boxes on a form,
Something that allows me not to conform.
Some think of me as the product of a sin,
They wonder what kind of love a black and white could
    possibly fall in.
There must be something wrong, something can't be right,
When two people are in love, one being black and the other
    white.
This must be wrong when blacks and whites find love,
This can't be all right with the man up above.
Don't call me an Oreo or a half-breed,

Give me the respect that I deserve and need.
Don't condemn me for the race I just happen to be,
Race is a small part of me.
Remember that people are a lot like books,
The outside shows little more than looks.
Prejudging may cost you a friend for life,
It may even cost you a husband or wife.
So next time you sit and attempt to categorize,
Remember there's more than meets the eyes.

By **BRIAN HARRIS,** fourteen (when written);
this poem was originally published
in *New People* magazine.

"In the United States, you can't just be a little black," concludes
G. Reginald Daniel, a sociologist at the University of California at
Santa Barbara, who has studied and taught classes about multiracial identity. "You either are or you aren't." If you are a mixed-
race person of black and white heritage, for example, you are
simply black, never white or mixed race.

Daniel, who is multiracial, points out that this "makes no sense
logically because if you have just one African forebear, you, and
every descendant of yours for infinity, are going to be identified as
African-American." This type of thinking has been referred to as
the "one-drop rule." It has existed in this country, formally (by
law) and informally, for hundreds of years.

The one-drop rule has been used to oppress African-Americans.
During slavery, slave owners classified all mixed-race children of
a white person and a black person—mostly slave masters and
slave women—as slaves, and this increased the slave force.

Today, oddly enough, some of the staunchest supporters of one-drop thinking are African-Americans themselves. They are also some of the people who have expressed the most opposition to the inclusion of a multiracial identifier on the census or other official recognition of mixed-race people.

One of the reasons that African-Americans take this stance is that having more people who identify as African-American increases their numbers and power base as they struggle to get some of the rights and opportunities that have been denied them because of racism. The fear is that people who claim a racially mixed identity would no longer label themselves African-American.

As a result, multiracial people, like Tiger Woods, who identify themselves as multiracial, rather than simply as black, are often labeled self-hating traitors and sellouts by African-Americans.

But many of the racially mixed people I interviewed who have a black heritage experience the pressure to identify as just African-American as extremely coercive and hurtful. While being proud of their black heritage, they don't want to deny the other parts of themselves. Furthermore, many consider themselves to be both African-American and mixed race, and they don't want to choose one or the other.

Professor Daniel thinks the struggle for racially mixed people with black heritage is to be allowed to claim these other, nonblack parts of themselves. But the struggle for multiracial people with Native American ancestry is almost the opposite—that is, many of them must fight to be allowed to claim their Native American part.

What defines an Indian? Is it blood quantum—the amount of "Indian blood" someone has? Is it growing up on a reservation? Is it knowing the culture and traditions? This is a controversial issue among Native Americans today.

I DON'T THINK PEOPLE SHOULD HAVE TO PROVE THEMSELVES

Denise (left) with her friend Anna Tsoublarakis, who is Greek and Navajo.

DENISE HOBSON, twenty
Chinle, Arizona
Mother: Navajo
Father: European-American (Anglo-Irish)

I grew up on the Navajo reservation in northeastern Arizona. My mother is Navajo and my father is of Irish descent from Manhattan. My dad's family moved out west to work at a Japanese relocation camp in Idaho, and then his parents got teaching positions on the Navajo reservation. They lived there for over thirty years and that's where my dad grew up—less than sixty miles from where my mother lived her whole life.

It was pretty dull on the reservation. The Navajo reservation is very desolate—there are not a lot of businesses. Our tribe doesn't want a lot of white-owned businesses taking over more of our land. When I last lived in Chinle year-round, we had one supermarket, one fast-food place—Kentucky Fried Chicken—and two gas stations. The big thing was getting a stop light at one of our major crossings. As small as it is, our town is one of the bigger towns on the reservation.

My Navajo grandmother and even my mother and her sisters are into sheepherding and weaving. Navajo rugs are popular items for the tourists. That's the main source of income for a lot

65

of traditional older women. A lot of men are farmers. But it's not good farming land; it's dry and can get really windy. The crops are grown just to support the farmers' families.

The boarding school system employs a lot of Native people now. The U.S. government started these federal boarding schools on the reservations years ago. They are good schools these days, but they used to be horrible institutions, especially for young children. Before, it was mainly white people who tried to make the Indian kids "act white." Now most of the schools are very pro-Indian and promote Indian culture and the Navajo language.

My grandmother went to a boarding school when they were first set up. That was when they were trying to assimilate Native people into white culture. They tried to set up the boarding schools far from communities so that kids couldn't go home. They tried to remove them from the culture as much as possible.

My grandma had her hair cut very short and she wasn't allowed to speak Navajo. It is bad luck to cut a young girl's hair like that. She has a lot of sad and bitter memories about that experience. They tried to erase her culture but she retained everything she knew in her heart. She is such a strong woman. It's hard for me to think of what my grandmother and even my mother had to go through just to get an education.

School was difficult, because when I was really little I was teased a lot. First and second grades were pretty bad. Little boys would call me names in Navajo. They always chanted "*bi-lasáana*," which means "white apple," literally, you're red on the outside but you're white on the inside. It's kind of funny now to look back on how those kids tried to hurt me. My grandma taught me and my siblings Navajo words so we could stand up for ourselves.

When I was in junior high school I didn't hang out with Native people, especially on the reservation. I really stood out; I do not "look Native." I was pretty much considered white. There were a few of us in the whole school who were mixed, both Navajo and white, and there were about five white students in my whole class. We had our own little clique. We all got teased. After a while, we didn't pay attention to it and it wore off by sixth grade. By the time we got to the eighth grade, we were a fairly popular group.

After eighth grade, I went away to private schools in Massachusetts and New Hampshire. There weren't very many Native people there. I was considered the white kid when I was on the reservation, but when I went away to private school, I stood out among the whites as the Indian. I just couldn't fit in with the group I was with.

My parents pushed us to go away to New England because they wanted us to go to a good school. I'm really glad I got away when I did. A lot of people in the class I would have graduated with if I had stayed on the reservation have had kids and have become involved with drugs and alcohol. Only a few have gone on to college. For a lot of people who lived on the reservation their whole lives, it's very hard to leave.

The Navajo tribe is the largest tribe. The only larger tribe is maybe the Cherokee. We have a stricter blood quantum. We only go up to one-fourth Navajo blood. If you're one-eighth, you're not on the Navajo rolls. There are a lot of people out there who are one-eighth or one-sixteenth Navajo who grew up on the reservation and live very traditional lives, but can't be "official" Navajos.

I don't know how I feel about the whole blood quantum thing. It bothers me that there are Navajos who grew up on the reservation but they can't be considered Navajo. But it's hard to say that someone who's one-sixty-fourth Indian is really traditional, especially if their tribe doesn't have a reservation.

It's a concern for me because my oldest sister is married and has a daughter and a son. My mom is very traditional and has been teaching the kids a lot of Navajo words and traditions. So they are having a Navajo upbringing. But they are only a quarter Navajo. So if they don't marry people who are at least a quarter Navajo as well, their kids won't be considered Navajo. And that's kind of sad to think about because it seems like our culture could slowly wither away. But that is in terms of blood quantum. In my mind, traditions and culture are what make you who you are.

We have this debate at Dartmouth, too, within our own little Native American group. There are probably a hundred fifty enrolled Native students. I came in as a freshman thinking that Dartmouth had the highest Native population and that I was going to fit in this time. So I was really excited.

But I felt like I had to pass this test before I was accepted. "Do you know your language?" "Do you know your traditions?" "Do you know your culture?" "Do you dress traditionally?" "Do you go to powwows?" I heard these questions every time I met another Native student.

I heard comments like, "Your skin is really light." "You don't sound like you're Indian. You don't have an accent, you don't have a twang."

And I was thinking, "I grew up on a reservation. I grew up in a traditional lifestyle. What more do you want me to tell you to prove who I am?"

It seemed like there was this checklist of what you needed in order to be Indian here. That was so strange to me because I was expecting to be embraced by this Native community and then I was kind of pushed away, as if I was not Indian enough for them. My first friend at Dartmouth, Anna, who's Navajo and Greek, was immediately accepted. Maybe it was because she is dark and has long hair and she loves going to powwows. We are a lot alike, but because we look a little different in color, we are judged differently.

The funny thing is that a lot of the people who did that to me were also in the same position I'm in—they came from mixed backgrounds. Many of the Native students here are mixed too. Because they want to prove that they're more Indian than you are, a lot of people don't talk about their white background. The first thing that comes out of their mouths is, "Yeah, I'm Indian and proud!"

But I always say, "I'm half Navajo and I'm half white and I'm proud!" I have always acknowledged both cultures, because I always acknowledge both of my parents. I respect their differences, and their differences are what make me a whole person.

I remember we were having this conversation once at the Native American Affinity House. There were three of us; we were all half Native American and something else. This older girl was telling this guy, "You are not Indian because you don't know your language. What are you going to pass on to your children? You can't just pass on your Indian blood. You have to know your culture—this is what makes you Indian. You have to know your tradition, your history, and some of your language."

I said, "What if you are full-blooded Indian, but you grew up in the city and you don't know your language and your culture? Does that make you Indian?"

She said, "Yeah, that makes you Indian. You can be full blooded. Or you can be a mixed blood as long as you know all this other traditional stuff."

69

So I said, "My father grew up on the reservation. He knows all the Navajo traditions. He speaks the Navajo language and he's married to a Navajo woman. He respects the Navajo ways of life. So does that make him Indian?"

She said yeah. And I said, "My dad's white. Does that make him Indian?"

She's like, "Oh, no, no, no, no, no, no. You have to have some Indian blood."

I said, "But he's passed your checklist. Aren't you saying he is more Indian than me 'cause he knows more than I do?"

People don't really know what they are talking about, I guess. It's tough to say who is Indian and who is not. I don't think I should be more Indian than anyone else. I don't think people should have to prove themselves.

But at the same time, I don't know why people want to be Indian if they don't know anything about it. And I guess that's why Native people question one another: "Are you really Indian? Are you trying to be something that you're not?"

People want to say they're Indian and they want to know about Indian culture. They have a romantic view of Indian people, so they want to pretend they're Indian to reach some spiritual state. They want to do ceremonies and sweat lodges and all this stuff that a lot of Indian people don't even do. They don't understand the power and strength of these ceremonies and they play around pretending to be cultural, and that can be viewed as disrespectful.

A lot of people say, "Well, what makes you Indian?" You can't *be* Indian. You just are if you are. It's not something that you have to aspire to be or try to prove. It just is. You don't have to separate yourself into "I'm half Navajo and I'm half white." There is no separation. It's something that you are and you were brought up with.

I'm Indian. But there are a lot of things about me that are from my Anglo-Irish background. My Native self, my white self—they are two different elements, but they make me one, they make me whole. Navajos believe that we must all walk in beauty—and we can only do that if we have balance within ourselves and an understanding of each other.

IF YOU'RE ASIAN, THEY JUST CALL YOU CHINESE

Ches, wearing a cap, clowns around with his older brother, Soul.

CHESTER EVANS, twenty-one
Tokyo, Japan
Mother: Japanese, Chinese
Father: European-American

I feel really fortunate that I had a chance to meet my mother's family and live six years in Japan and go to school there. I felt so comfortable living in Japan. It was just like having both my worlds in one place.

Being in the military, we got the American environment on the base, then we went out the gates to our other side. The Japanese treated us like celebrities. Japanese kids would come up to us and touch us and say, "*Gaijin, gaijin* [foreigner]."

When I lived in Japan I think mixed families were the majority on the military bases. I went to Yokota High School and I'd say at

71

least half, if not more, of the school was Amerasian or mixed. Race wasn't just a black and white issue.

I remember when we took our SATs in high school and they asked us for our race. They didn't have an Amerasian box. They had "other," but I thought that was kind of offensive or degrading. Because I went to school with a lot of Amerasians, we'd complain, "How come they've always got black, white, Asian, or Hispanic, and there's nothing about mixed Asians?"

So I always put Asian-American. I am proud of my Japanese heritage. Not that I'm not proud of my dad's heritage—it's just that I think people are going to look at me as an Asian more than they're going to look at me as a white person.

When I graduated I went straight to Alabama—the University of South Alabama. I'd been to Alabama to visit my grandmother and I felt pretty comfortable going there. But it really didn't work out for me. I couldn't live in Alabama.

In the South, it's just strictly black and white. It's like you have to identify with either group—there's no in-between. Coming from the military community, that was weird. I saw no Amerasians. I think I was the only Amerasian in the whole school.

In the South, they're surprised that I'm Japanese. When they think of the Japanese, they think of a full-blooded Japanese person. And down in the South, out in the country, they call anybody who's not black "white" pretty much. If you're Asian, they just call you Chinese.

People who were born and raised in Alabama would be like, "You're not from here."

I'd be like, "No, I'm from Japan."

Then they'd say, "Oh, really? You don't look like Bruce Lee."

And that didn't offend me. I just said, "Well, I'm not related to him either."

There were a couple of incidents. When my brother lived in Alabama—he was in second grade or third grade—a group of white boys tied a rope around his neck and called him "Chinese boy" and "gook" and stuff like that. That was back in the seventies. I never had anything as dramatic as that happen to me, but I've had people call me "gook" or "half-breed."

During spring break '95, I drove down to Panama City, Florida, with my friends for the weekend. We were walking the strip trying to find a hotel, and this big truck with a Confederate flag flying drove by. The people inside the truck threw beer cans at us and called us "nigger."

A lot of people say that things have changed in the South since thirty years ago and if you come down here today people are really friendly. But being mixed race, you can still see it. You see how people interact. You go anyplace—like any restaurant anywhere—and the black people work in the back and the white people work up front. And people don't realize that because it's been the normal thing since the beginning of time down here. I don't think a lot of the black people even realize it. But coming from a mixed society, I'm like, "Damn!"

I feel more comfortable around a military environment than a civilian one. The racial mixture of the military environment is a lot more diverse. You don't see a lot of segregation. You all work in the same places. You all go to the same schools. You all live in the same neighborhoods.

I left the University of South Alabama and I joined the military. I was hoping to get out of the South, but they sent me straight to Mississippi. I stayed in Mississippi for a year and then I got orders to go to South Carolina. I've been here for two years in Charleston. It's really black and white down here too. The only Asians you see in Charleston are affiliated with the base. **73**

I never had a problem with being mixed until now. Growing up in Japan, I never had to worry about it because the majority of people I was around were mixed people. But now, being in a black and white society, I'm so conscious of it. Every day when I look in the mirror, that's the first thing that pops into my head. I'm always worried about how people are going to look at me. Are they going to accept me for what or who I am? It's not a problem within myself—it's a problem with how people look at me.

Three years ago I went to San Francisco to see a friend. There's a lot of racial diversity over there. I saw all of these Asian people. It was just such a comfortable feeling. I didn't want to leave, you know. California—that's where I want to go when I get out of the military.

Racially mixed people who move from the West Coast to the East Coast, the suburbs to the city, or even from one small town to another will often find that the way others view or categorize them changes. Young people may experience this when they move away from home to attend college or start a new job.

The bad news is that, if you've worked out a racial identity that you are comfortable with and that your community supports, you may find yourself in a new community that does not see you in the same way, says psychologist Maria Root. For example, Chester, who was comfortable while living on a military base in Japan, where Asians and interracial families were common, feels self-conscious in parts of the South, where race is defined much more rigidly and in black and white terms.

But the good news, says Root, is that, if you don't like the way 74 *people categorize or view you in the place you live now, when you are old enough to be on your own you can relocate to a more ac-cepting place. "It may make you feel a whole lot more at ease and congruent with yourself." Laura, the next person you'll meet, did just that.*

A SQUARE PEG IN A ROUND HOLE

LAURA,* eighteen
Michigan
Mother: European-American
Father: Hawaiian, Spanish, Filipino, Chinese

In Hawaii, I knew who was Filipino, who was Japanese, who was Chinese, who was like me, who was white. Yet we were all comfortable talking to each other. We didn't even think about who a person's parents were, we were just friends. If there was a Filipino festival, it was just known over there that you didn't have to be Filipino to go. You grow up different.

We left Hawaii when I was ten. When I got here, I enrolled in this really small Catholic school. Everyone was white. After a while, they started calling me "Hawaiian Punch" and "China eyes" and "foreigner." I had never encountered this before. So I would go home and I would tell my mom. I don't think she really wanted to believe that they were teasing me because of the way I looked, so she told me they were just being little kids and that if I was chubby they would tease me about that, and if I had glasses they would tease me about that.

My senior year in high school, I moved to a new school. I was the only Asian girl there and probably one of the only Asians they

75

had ever seen. *Pocahontas* [the movie] was coming out. They never even bothered to figure out what my name was, they just called me Pocahontas.

And that was when I figured out what people were really teasing me about. Because here I am at a brand-new school, and these people don't know who I am, and they are calling me this because they think I look Indian. Even after I was there for a while and I had made friends, they still called me Pocahontas, they never called me Laura. So then I figured out that when I was little they were teasing me just because of the way I looked. So I got mad. I stayed mad my whole senior year.

Where I lived, they just couldn't accept me as one of these small-town Michigan girls. When I first got there, everyone had their hair to their shoulders and permed and they curled their bangs and frizzed them all up. I had the Asian long flat hair so that was different. All I wanted to be was just another kid and I was never going to be that. I had this label put on me because of the way I look.

I got so sick and tired of trying to fit in. And I finally got to the point where I accepted that I was not going to be one of them. So I was like, "Fine, trying to fit in is not going to work—I will just totally not fit in." So I stopped dressing like all of my peers and I went off and did my own California-Hawaii thing. I just wore surf clothes—baggy pants and really oversized T-shirts. And I dressed like that for a while. So then I was comfortable.

My mom calls me a square peg in a round hole. She says, "I don't think you'll ever fit."

About nine months after we talked, I got an e-mail from Laura.
76 *Here's what she wrote:*

"Hiya! Well, guess what? I am back home again! Yup, I transferred for spring '98 and now I am living with a friend from Guam. I applied to UH [University of Hawaii] with a friend who was from Maui and also hated Michigan. I got accepted and I sold my car, got on a plane and I am here. My mom says I am wasting my education and losing focus. But in Michigan I was so unhappy. Here I am content and I am so happy. It is unbelievable!"

Hawaii has a long history of racial mixing, starting with the marriages of whites with Hawaiian royalty hundreds of years ago. More than one-third—or 37 percent—of the population of this state is multiracial, and another 37.5 percent are Asian/Pacific Islanders. At about 23 percent, whites are a minority, according to "The Health Surveillance," the 1992 Hawaii State Department of Health Survey. It's a comfortable place for many kinds of mixed-race people.

Communities of people who identify as racially mixed have existed in the United States for hundreds of years, says Reginald Daniel, although most of us have never heard about them. Daniel has studied and written about some of these groups in which there has been generation after generation of racial mixing. Over time, each of these enclaves created its own "mixed" reality—a distinct culture, history, and tradition. The Creoles of Color and the Black Seminoles are two of these communities.

DOWN HERE IT'S CALLED CREOLE

LESLIE THIBODEAUX, sixteen
Lake Charles, Louisiana
Mother: Creole
Father: Creole

I have white, black, Spanish, and Indian in me. Down here it's called Creole. Basically, it's a mixture of different races—especially white, black, Spanish, and Indian.

Louisiana was always known to be a prejudiced state and Creole heritage had not been accepted by a lot of people. Not many people even know what it is. There's a Creole language—it's broken-down French. It's not the same as regular true French, but the meanings are very close. My mom and dad speak it—pretty much everybody in my family does.

We're known for the spicy foods. Gumbo is a Creole food. So is rice dressing, or dirty rice—that's what my mom calls it. Red beans and rice, red beans and sausage, crawfish—those are just some of the foods that we eat.

A lot of my family members don't look like me. Some of them look a lot different. On my mom's side of the family, people have the straight hair, the blond and red hair color, and the blue eyes.

And on my dad's side, people have the darker skin and different hair textures.

On my birth certificate, it says I'm black. When I was really young, I can remember when my mom signed me up for school. There was this form with the boxes for race and ethnic background. They only had spaces for black, white, or Hispanic. My mom put black on there and the woman was like, "Are you sure this is right?" because I had the long straight hair, and the pale, pale skin, and the hazel-green eyes.

It's upsetting that they don't have a space for mixed heritage or multicultural heritage. It's kind of hard because if you have that little percentage of black heritage from way back and you have all these other heritages, black is put on the transcript. There is no in-between. And when I put down a certain background, like black, for instance, people look at me kind of strange. I'd get the weird looks and the stares. People look at me like I'm totally different from anybody else and it kind of makes me feel bad. Why do they stare and make it so noticeable that they're curious about that?

Growing up, I always got the questions, "What are you?" "What's your background?" and "What nationality are you?" And it was kind of hard to explain exactly what my background was and some people didn't believe it when I did. A lot of people don't know what the definition of Creole is and it takes a while to explain it to them. Sometimes you want to tell them to mind their own business.

People would ask, "Who was that?" and they wouldn't believe that it was a family member sometimes. Or they'd see my mom or my dad and they'd be like, "Is your mom white and is your dad black?" And it's hard to have to explain it's because my mom and dad are also of mixed heritage. My mom looks white but my dad **79** does not. My father has a darker skin complexion. In Louisiana, most people dislike interracial couples. My parents don't really notice the weird looks that people give them. But when I'm with them, I notice the looks.

I talked to my parents about it and they said it was worse when they were growing up because that was before the civil rights movement and blacks were supposed to stay in their corner and whites were supposed to stay on the other side. On their birth certificates they were black, so both of my parents stayed in the black areas from the time they were kids until segregation ended. My mother and father were taught that no matter what you looked like, it was best to stay on your side or you could get into a lot of trouble.

They told me a lot of stories. There was a "whites only" water fountain and a "blacks only" water fountain. They told me that there was a certain section reserved for each race in restaurants, and how they sometimes had to go in through the back door. I can remember my mom telling me that there was even a white section and a black section in the doctor's office. Once she was sitting in the black section and one of the nurses pulled her over and said, "You know, you're sitting in the wrong section," and moved her to the white area.

And it was really tough back then because people would look at you weird if you had the light skin and the light eyes and the straight hair and you said you were of black heritage. It was a lot worse back then, but it's still bad in this day and age.

Some people who are multicultural or Creole sometimes feel uncomfortable telling people that they are. Because of their looks they can get away with telling people that they're white. What is so degrading, even though I am of Creole descent, is that some people in my family don't choose to identify themselves with my family. They want to take that route as only being white.

But I don't think that people who have straight hair and blue eyes and pale, pale skin are African-Americans. A lot of them want to be known as Creole. And blacks are like, "They have black in them, they should say they are black. They're just trying to get out of it by making up Creole," which is not true at all. It's not fair to people who have more than one nationality in them to say that they are black no matter what else they have in them. And I guess people of mixed heritage or Creole heritage are starting to get tired of it. They want their heritage to be known.

They have the black heritage festival and the Irish festival, and they just started having the Creole heritage festival in Natchitoches. I haven't had an opportunity to go, but a bunch of my family members went and they said you would never know that there are so many people like us in Louisiana. Once they all come together, you realize that you're not the only one.

"WE ARE BLACK INDIANS"

KEVIN MAILLARD, twenty-four
Tulsa, Oklahoma
Mother: Black Indian
Father: African-American

My mother is from Wewoka, Oklahoma. That's the capital of the Seminole Nation and that's what our tribe is. People from both sides of her family have been mixing race—African-American and **81**

Native American—for hundreds of years. They're called Black Seminoles.

Most of my mom's side of the family came up from Florida. I don't know how much of this to believe, but I heard that there was this woman whose father was a chief of some Seminole tribe in Florida. After he died, his daughter rode up on the Trail of Tears.* The man who led her horse was this black man. They fell in love, had this family, and that's when the whole mixed side of the family began.

There isn't a Seminole reservation. It's just the Seminole Nation and it's like a big county. When they arrived in Oklahoma, a lot of people were allotted land. Everyone lives on these big farms with lots of horses and ponds and barns and chickens and geese. I remember running for hours and still being on our property; it's been in our family forever and ever. I spent my summers there.

Wewoka is actually this really interesting mixed town. It's in the middle of nowhere. There are probably about 5,000 people who live there and everyone is related in some really scary way. It's a Southern town so there is this main street that runs through it—one side is black and the other side is white. Indians and Black Indians live on the black side of town and all the white people live on the other. But people on both sides of this street are still related, anyway. There's so much intermingling.

The range in appearance of people is absolutely amazing—from people who look completely white to people who look like they stepped straight off the boat from Africa. Most Black Indians are visibly mixed. Like in my family all the women have long

---

*Between 1833 and 1858, the U.S. government forced about 3,000 Seminoles off their land in the Southeast and relocated them to Indian Territory, which is now Oklahoma. During these trips, which were made over land and water, an estimated 20 to 25 percent of the Seminoles died. The trek is sometimes referred to as the Trail of Tears. This phrase is most commonly used in association with the Cherokee, who lost 4,000 people when 15,000 of them were marched to Indian Territory in the 1830s.

straight hair and everyone has these funny cheeks and noses and lips. My mother definitely articulates herself as Black Indian. Most of the people within that community see themselves as mixed.

Anywhere from 30 percent to 70 percent of black people have some trace of Native American ancestry. A lot of people are like, "I had some Native American great-great-great-great-grandmother," or whatever. But people who identify themselves as Black Indians have a mental attachment to a mixed ancestry. There are whole generations of people who passed down their experiences and their life patterns as mixed people.

I think, for a lot of people who identify as just black, their parents identify as just black, so that whole idea of being mixed would have been lost a long, long time ago. But my mother's side of the family live in the Seminole Nation, so there's this constant reminder. It's like, "Seminole—that's what we are. We are Black Indians."

My father is African-American. I asked him who his grandparents were and what their race or ethnicity was and he didn't know. That's really weird because his mother looks white.

I knew that I was mixed because my mother told me all the time. She said, "Kevin, you are this and that, but people are going to see you as black, so you've got to deal."

I grew up in a conservative all-white town. There were probably about three or four other black kids at the high school I went to. The black kids lived in an apartment complex in a different area of town. There were a lot of issues that separated me from those kids.

Issues of race were ignored in general. I call it the Republican approach or the Reaganist approach to race—if you don't pay attention to it, it will go away. When race came up, it would be in English class when we were reading something like *To Kill a* **83**

Mockingbird. When we got to the part about Big Joe, I would feel heads turning to look at me and I just wanted to die in class. I would just wait for the teacher to say, "And what do you think, Kevin?"

A lot of people didn't know about my Indian background. They couldn't tell or they had these stereotypes of what Indian people looked like: They had really long spine-straight black hair and feathers stuck in the back of their heads and they rode horses to school and lived in tepees on reservations. They were all alcoholics and they were all poor.

Most all of my friends in high school were white and they would only see things as black and white. Everyone would see me as black with these Chicken George and Kunta Kinte qualities just coming out from everywhere. They would say really strange things like, "Since you have this really flat nose and this really dark skin and really big lips, isn't it hard for people to see you at night?" I'm not really dark and I don't have a really flat nose and I don't have really big lips. But people would assign all those characteristics to me anyway.

If I would mention something about going to the Seminole Nation or about being mixed, people would be like, "You're black, that's it."

I'd be like, "Oh, okay," because my friends were telling me this. But I just hated it when people said the word *black* or *white* or referred to me as black. I think a lot of my identity was shaped by people in high school because teenagers are always looking for acceptance and they just want to fit in. All I wanted was to not be seen as different. It was horrible.

It was hard growing up in this community—being black where there weren't many black people and being Indian where there weren't many Indian people and culturally growing up white. Later people would say, "You're not authentically black because you didn't grow up in the 'hood" or "You're not Indian because you didn't grow up on a reservation."

I went to Duke as an undergraduate and there was a Native American group and I remember thinking, "I don't know if I'd feel comfortable joining this organization because my face wouldn't look that Native American." At the same time, I didn't want to join the Black Students Association because some of my facial features didn't look that black. And then the way that I talk was white and a lot of things that I do were white, so I wouldn't wholly fit into any of these groups. So I ended up not joining any of those groups in college and doing student government instead.

There is a strong Native American community here at [the University of] Michigan. A lot of the people grew up on reservations in these really cold places like northern Wisconsin and Canada. I felt a lot of economic separation from them. We'd be at a party and they'd say, "Oh, Kevin, you're learning what it's like to be around Indian women." If you're part white, you're a mixed blood. If you're mixed with black, you're just black. Black overpowers every other culture you have.

The thing that makes me maddest is people telling me I'm not Indian. I remember this time with my roommate. I had just gotten my scholarship incentive money. If you're Indian and you made good grades, you got a couple hundred dollars for the term. I ended up using my money to go skiing with my friends, because that was the whole point—if you did well, you got this money.

He told me, "You shouldn't be using your money like that, because, first of all, you're not Indian. And second of all, if you were **85** really Indian, you should be using that money to buy clothes or shoes because most Indians are really poor."

I thought, "I have just as much right to this as anyone else who got it and it's my decision what to use it for."

It's a three-pronged thing—you're not black, you're not white, you're not Indian. It comes from all directions.

I'M BLACK AND KOREAN

As a child, Donna enjoyed dressing up in traditional Korean clothing. She is shown with her mother and stepfather, Yong and Ivan Wayman.

DONNA MAKETA RANDOLPH, twenty
Colorado Springs, Colorado
Mother: Korean-American
Stepfather: European-American
Biological Father: African-American

Colorado Springs is a military town. We're surrounded on almost every single side by some sort of military base. A lot of the students who went to school with me were biracial. Their parents met in their respective countries and then they settled here.

My parents met in Korea. My mother is Korean. My real father was in the army. They got married, then they came here. But they separated when I was three and divorced when I was six.

I have very little recollection of my real father. He was always away in the field or overseas. I didn't see him for months at a time, so I never really felt close to him. I think that's one of the reasons why it wasn't a big deal for me when they actually got divorced.

But it was a very hard thing for my mother, because her family wasn't too happy with the fact that she had married an American black. So she couldn't go back to Korea. Plus, she didn't have the money to go back.

She never got to finish high school in Korea. And when she came here, she obviously didn't have a degree of any kind. She didn't speak a lot of English. So she worked at a restaurant for a while. Her next job was at KP, which was basically cleaning up the mess halls—the dining halls for the military.

When I was seven, my mother remarried. My stepfather is who I consider to be my father. He's really the only father I've ever had.

My real father married a German woman and they have two daughters. So technically I have stepsiblings. But I've never met them. He wrote me probably twice.

I always thought I was more Korean than anything else. That's because my grandparents came to live with us for a little while, so there was a lot of Korean culture in my family—holidays and meals and things like that. I ate Korean foods a lot. We'd have rice almost every day and *kim chi* [pickled cabbage]. And my mom always had these strange Asian concoctions that she'd come up with when we were sick.

My grandmother was really sweet. I liked her and I respected her a lot. Obviously she was fluent in Korean; she didn't speak anything else. She started working and picked up a lot of English words and I picked up a lot of Korean words and that was enough for us—we found a way to get past the language barrier.

Before my grandmother came, my mother never really taught me anything about Korean culture. When she spoke Korean, it was to her friends only. She felt that she'd had such a hard time because she didn't know how to speak English. So she figured that it would be better if I just learned English.

Now my mom speaks English very well—she has very little accent. But sometimes when she talks, it doesn't come out quite right. I'm so used to it that it doesn't really bother me. But when I bring my friends over, sometimes they will be like, "What'd she say?" And if people use big words or speak really fast, she has a little bit of trouble.

My mom relies on me a lot. I'm like her dictionary. I make phone calls for her. I call insurance companies if there's a problem. I set up doctor's appointments, dentist's appointments. When we get legal documents or anything important like that, she has me read them and explain them to her.

Now my mom works at an assembly plant; they make locks. Technically, she doesn't have to work. She could live off what my stepfather makes or she could work part-time. She told me, "Well, the only reason I'm still working is because I want to get you through college."

I go to school at Cornell University. When I get out of Cornell, I'm going to get a decent job. College is a big thing in this family. I was expected to go, actually pushed, especially by my mother. She told me that she didn't want me to have a life like hers. It's funny because when I talk to my Korean friends they say their mothers push education too. We say, "Korean mothers are *sooo* strict." We Koreans know what that means.

Cornell is known for its diversity. But if you look around, you'll notice that black people hang with black people, and Asians hang with Asians, and whites hang with whites. This was very new to me.

In high school, obviously black people would mainly hang out together, but then I'd always see one or two white people or a couple of Hispanics with them. I saw a lot of biracial people who were Asian and white, a lot of people who were black and German or black and white. There were about six or seven people who were black and Korean at my school. So it wasn't like I was any different from anyone else. I never had any problems with what I was, never worried about it, never even thought about it.

One of the things I learned at Cornell is that you almost have to choose who you are—and I didn't want to do that. Obviously, if you look at me, I'm dark. I guess you'd relate to me as a black person. But I'm not black. For most of the black people at Cornell, I am a little too light. But with Asian people, I'm too dark. So I don't get acknowledged on either side.

There's actually a very strong Asian community at Cornell—it's about 20 percent Asian. It's interesting to watch them walk by; I just don't exist to them for the most part. For example, they have a society called the Korean Students' Association and they throw parties—big dances and whatever. I went once and people were looking at me like, "What's she here for? Who's she with? Why's she here?"

For the most part, people have no idea that I'm half Korean. I took a Korean-language class and we were talking about mixed-race children. One guy was talking about children who are white and Asian, which is fairly common. And I said, "Yeah, well, there's black and Korean too."

And this Korean girl looked directly across the table at me and said, "What!?" Her attitude really bothered me. It was like she was amazed that I was black and Korean—that there was a black and Korean woman in her presence. But what was also behind it was like, "That's not even possible. Why would any Korean woman marry a black male?" It seemed like she was shocked that such a thing even existed, that such an "abomination" even existed.

When I was growing up, a lot of the Korean women would look down on me. I would go with my mother when she would see her friends. Most of them were Korean women who were married to Asian men, most predominantly Korean, or they were married to white men. I never liked being stared at, and I always felt I was being stared at. A lot of these women would look at me as if they were thinking, "Okay, well, obviously her mother slept with a black guy or something." And then after that, they were like, "Okay, we've got to keep an eye on our stuff." That's how I always felt.

It doesn't happen anymore because all my mother has to say is, "My daughter is going to Cornell and she's doing really well." And they'll go, "Ohh," and that basically means, "Oh, well then, that's okay."

Koreans are very prejudiced. Now that I've learned a little bit about Korean history, I understand why. They were always being taken over by some foreign invader or another, so their feeling is, "Now we just want to be Korean. We just want to have Korean bloodlines."

When I took my Korean class last year we were doing a section on race, like how you'd say, "I am American" or "I am Korean" or whatever. And I raised my hand and I said, "What do you call someone who's mixed?" And my teacher, who was Korean, goes, "Well, uh, uh, well, this is the word," and she told me, "but it's not a very good word." And so it's not a good thing to be mixed.

I feel that I've had to prove a lot of things because I'm mixed. Like I've met my [step]father's family and they're all white. They're all blond-haired and blue-eyed. And I think that if I do something weird they're going to look at me like, "Oh, my God—all of those Koreans!" or "Oh, my God—all of those black people!" And I don't want that.

Because I've got two cultures in me—actually I've got three because my stepfather is white—I have to be open-minded and respect all of them. I can't listen to really radical black people say whites are bad, because my father is white. I can't listen to white people say black people are lazy, because my biological father is black. I can't listen to people say that Koreans are exotic, or that they're just really smart and have nothing else to them, because I'm part Korean.

I'm lucky. I come from a really stable family. I think my mom raised me well. Both my parents provided me with a very comfortable atmosphere to be in. My mom was always there to talk to. Granted we've had our conflicts—but I love my mom a lot. My friends tease me because I'm always talking about how much I love my mom and how I want to be there for her.

I think the reason why I'm so close to her is because we did depend on each other so much. She was my only parent and she was the one who raised me. When I had to learn my multiplication tables in the third grade, she was the one who sat down with me and helped me. She's always been there for me.

She told me that right after she left my father she really got down about things. She just basically stopped caring about herself. She felt, "I'm here in this country. I don't have a job or an education. I can't go home. Oh, my life is over." What made her turn back and realize, "No, I can't do this," was me. Her feelings were, "I have this daughter and I can't let her down."

I know how much she's sacrificed for me. I just can't help but respect her for that. And I can't help but love her for that.

What's life like inside an interracial family? What are the difficulties? What are the rewards? And how do these families deal with the racial and cultural differences under their roofs, as well as help their children cope with the prejudices of the outside world?

Maria Root has recently completed a five-year study of 200 interracial families, described in her book Love's Revolution: Racial Intermarriage *(Temple University Press, 1999). "There is such variety in these families," she says.*

"On one end of the spectrum, you have families where parents are wonderful—they're good guides, they listen well, they don't feel like they need to know it all but they have the basics in place." And on the other end, "you have parents who don't have the skills to negotiate family life, communication, conflict, much less the racial terrain."

WE ARE JUST THE BRADY BUNCH—KIND OF

MARIA BARNER, twenty-one
Norfolk, Virginia
Mother: European-American
Father: African-American

I never think of race as an issue. My mom is white and my dad is black—they're just Mom and Dad. It hasn't been a big deal.

I have a younger sister and four older brothers, but they're half brothers—two white and two black. They are my mom's two sons from her previous marriage and my dad's two sons from his previous marriage. We are just the Brady Bunch—kind of.

We're not an uptight family. When Gary, my youngest brother, who is white, was in high school, he was dating this white girl. They were driving somewhere and she saw a black and white couple on the sidewalk—this black guy and white girl. And she said, "Oh, God, look at that! That is so disgusting! How can she be with a black man? She can do so much better."

Being the cool family that we are, my brother was like, "Okay, whatever." So he picked her up the next day and he brought her over here and introduced her to our dad. She was so embarrassed; her face was bright red. Of course, that ended it.

I've been living in this neighborhood my whole life and it's predominantly upper-class black. Most of my friends have been black because that's who we've been around. In elementary school I remember my sister getting into fights all the time with little boys. They would call us names—"Oreo" and "zebra" and stuff like that. But they were just little kids. Kids can be cruel. I called people names too.

I never had any problems in high school. My high school was predominantly black. I never really experienced any racism until I got to college. There were a lot of negative feelings toward interracial relationships and black people. I was a lot more accepted by the black community than by whites. But a lot of black people had a real problem with black men dating white women. A lot of black athletes dated white girls. And then there were black girls dating white guys.

My brother Paul and his friend came to visit me just before I graduated and they're both white. The black frat has parties on campus and I took them to one. My brother is dark—he has a darker complexion, he has dark hair—but he's still white. And his friend was just as white as you can be. They looked like undercover police officers.

95

So when I walked in with them, all my black friends were like, "What's wrong with you? Who's that?"

I said, "This is my brother."

Everybody was like, "All right, that's cool."

But I didn't walk around with a sign, "This is my brother, don't be alarmed." So after we left there, he told me that the black guys were saying stuff to him. He said, "They were real rude there."

Then we went to a club on campus that was black-owned. When I was walking off the dance floor, this black guy I didn't know grabbed my arm, and said, "Hey, I know you're not with that cracker."

I was shocked. So I told everyone, "Let's leave."

I take Gary to work all the time. We always stop at 7-Eleven and get something to drink, and people always look. They always stare. I get that all the time when I go out with my brother.

I've learned how to deal with the staring—I don't go off the deep end or get mad. When I was younger, my mom would notice stuff like that. People would say stuff like, "That can't be your daughter."

I remember when we went to my sister's; her boyfriend had a cookout. His family was all black. My mom was talking to some lady and I was sitting beside her, and my mom said, "This is my daughter Maria."

She was like, "This is your daughter?" And then she tried to catch herself because it looked like she wanted to say something. Then she said, "Oh, she doesn't look anything like you." I looked at my mom and started laughing because it's just funny how uncomfortable people get.

I think the reason my sister and I are so laid-back about the whole "biracial issue" is because my parents were always very open and honest with us. We could talk about anything and everything, and still do. We're always loose and open. We never let people get to us.

THEIR EYES WOULD BUG OUT

JENNIFER HO, twenty-four
Oakland, California
Mother: European-American (English, French, Irish, Scottish)
Father: Chinese-American

My skin tone was darker when I was younger, so I definitely looked much darker than my mother. She's blond and she has blue-green eyes and she's very fair. She says people would come up to her and say, "Oh, what a beautiful baby! Whose is it?"

She would say, "She's mine," and they would look at her like she was lying or something.

Last year I went to China with my father. We visited some universities and I got to interact with students. They wanted to see an American their age. I would be introduced as my father's daughter and they would gasp. Their eyes would bug out. They would look at him, then they would look at me, then they would look back at him, and then they would look back at me. You could just see them struggling to put this together.

WE DIDN'T LOOK RELATED

INDIA,* twenty-three
Indiana
Mother: Native American, Black, White
Father: Native American, Black, White

My mom told me that when I was two or three years old we were in the department store. I was standing next to her. She was very tanned, it was summertime. I was very white-looking at the time. And these two little old women, who were white, walked up to me and said, "Oh, little girl, are you lost?" and they proceeded to take me away from my mom, who was looking at something on the rack.

My mom looked up and said, "That's my daughter!" My mom says I should have seen the looks on their faces. They looked at her in disbelief, as if it were impossible, because my mom was a whole different color than me and we didn't look related. People are funny sometimes.

WE HAVE CLOSED MOUTHS ON BOTH SIDES OF THE FAMILY

Sarah looks through a family scrapbook with her grandmother Sei Ichioka.

KAT WADE

SARAH ICHIOKA, seventeen
Berkeley, California
Mother: European-American
Father: Japanese-American

My mom's parents are really great and I think we're actually their favorite grandchildren, my brother and me. But when my mom was first going to marry my dad, they said, "You're going to have cultural problems, dear. It's just a passing phase."

The stereotype of interracial marriage is that it will never work out, that there will always be cultural differences. But I've had a really good life, as far as love and attention, and family life. I couldn't imagine growing up any other way.

On my mother's side of the family, almost all of my great-grandfather's family died in the Nazi concentration camps. Both sides of his family were Russian Jews. Only my great-grandfather and his sister survived and they had been a really big family. That's something that my grandfather doesn't talk about.

My dad's parents came to San Francisco from Japan. They were interned at Topaz* and my dad was born in the internment camp.

*Topaz, Utah, was one of many relocation centers that the U.S. government set up to house 110,000 Japanese-Americans during World War II, after forcing them from their homes and businesses. This policy is now regarded as an example of racial discrimination and a shameful episode in American history. Admitting that an injustice was committed, the U.S. government recently paid a restitution of $20,000 to each living survivor of the internment.

Before that, my grandfather ran a pretty successful import business. But during the internment, he had to leave his business, and it was gone when he came back. So the only job he could get was as a gardener, even though he had never gardened in his life, because everyone just kind of assumed that the Japanese were good at it. My grandma did cleaning and sewing for people.

Freshman year we had to do a living-history report. That was the first time I really talked to her about the internment. She was angry about it. She kept on mentioning how they had to sell their baby grand piano for some measly price. She focused all of her anger on that point. I hadn't known that they were staying in stables for a month before they got shipped to Topaz. That upset me a lot. It was painful for my grandmother, so she doesn't like to talk about it. We have closed mouths on both sides of the family.

I wish my dad had been born before that changing point. After the internment, they started speaking English at home. It was like, "Let's be really American. We're never going to let this happen to us again. We're not going to stick out at all." So my dad only has a junior high school level of Japanese whereas his older siblings are fluent and bilingual.

I would love to be bilingual. I wish I could communicate more with my grandmother. I wish we had more traditions in my family. Sometimes I just feel like I'm generic—I don't feel any strong ties to any one culture at all and I envy my friends who do. I think if I had more of the Japanese culture I would feel better about being identified as Asian. I'd feel more confident about it.

People usually just automatically assume that I'm Asian. After a long time, they'll be like, "Oh, you have green eyes. Are you wearing colored contacts?"

I'll say, "My mom's white."

100   And they'll say, "Ohh, okay." There's always that "Ohh, okay."

Back in February, I visited colleges on the East Coast. I drove around with my aunt and her two little children who live in Virginia. She's my mom's sister. I realized that when we stayed at hotels or went out to restaurants people thought I was maybe their au pair. There was no way they thought I could be related—I don't look anything like my aunt and those little blond curly-haired children. It was really weird—people would give us these looks trying to figure out what was going on. And I'm sure a little bit of it was just me being paranoid, but I really think that people did have a hard time figuring it out.

When I was younger and my aunt and I were really close, she said that I was the first person of color she thought of as just me and not as a person of color. I appreciated her honesty but she made me realize that people who don't meet me as a little baby in a close family relationship are going to put me in another category—that I'm not just Sarah first. You know, like in bad journalism when someone was arrested they'll write "so and so," comma, "black," when it's not necessary. Otherwise, if it's not stated, you just assume they were white. I think it was that kind of thing, like "so and so," comma, "Asian, my friend." You know, just a little mental category for people.

And another comment I remember from my childhood was from my grandmother on my mom's side. She said, "You look like such a beautiful Japanese princess." If it were my other cousin, I know she wouldn't have said, "Oh, you look like such a beautiful French princess." She would have just said, "Oh, you look like such a beautiful princess." That really was a distinction.

I remember my grandfather calling my dad and saying, "Oh, I wish I had your Japanese green thumb." My dad laughed about it later. Like there are these little comments they think are compliments but they have this kind of classification implicit in them. **101**

Race has been a difficult subject in my family lately. Last week I got into a big fight with my mom about how people classify other races. She thinks that stereotypes like "All Asians look alike" are just an inherent thing that people do and that they can't help it at all. But I think that you can definitely catch yourself and train yourself not to do it. So we got into a loud argument walking home from a restaurant.

She's a good person. We've always had such a close relationship that it never seemed like there could be something between us. But there's a big difference in how we deal with the world. I've just realized that recently.

I've had all of these realizations in the last two years. I feel like I've really started to grow and have my own opinions about things. I guess that's what this time of life is about—finding out who you really are.

THERE WAS RICE AT EVERY MEAL

Eric (second from the right) with his brother, Alan, and parents, Richard and Keiko.

ERIC KOJI STOWE, twenty-six
Sacramento, California
Mother: Japanese-American
Father: African-American

Among my friends' parents, my parents are one of the few couples who have lasted. My father is six foot six, 270 pounds, whereas my mom is five foot two and a little Asian woman. They've been married for thirty-four years. Yet they still go out to eat. They still laugh and they still hold hands. They still enjoy their time together. They're very cute.

When I was growing up, they were a great example of a relationship and a monogamous marriage. They provided for my brother and myself—we never had to struggle for anything because they made many sacrifices for us. I think my brother and I realize what they've done for us and what we have to do to pay them back, which is to be good sons.

Looking at my friends' households, I would say our household has more of an Asian influence. My father chose to learn the Japanese language and culture in order to get to know my mother and her family. That helped him get accepted in their society. So the Asian perspective, or the Asian philosophy, had more influ- **103** ence in our house. Although my dad made the rules, he was really soft-spoken and never had to yell at us, never hit us. That whole Asian "respect" thing was there.

A lot of the showing of love and affection in our household is done through actions. I think that's an example of the Asian influence. I look at some of my African-American friends and they give big hugs and say "I love you" to their parents. And some of them didn't understand the fact that I've only told my parents that I love them once. I respect them, and I do what they say, and that's how I show my love for them. It's just unspoken. We're definitely a lot tighter than some of my friends' families.

I chose to accept a lot of the Japanese philosophy and religion. I chose to cling to it and learn it. When I was growing up, we went to a Buddhist temple. But it wasn't until I got to college that I started reading a lot of the literature and philosophy. I learned Japanese, I kept that as a minor. I noticed how people are so quick to judge and lash out at other people. I try to keep an open mind and an open heart. Being raised a Buddhist and adhering to some of the philosophy, I think it was easier for me to accept other people.

There are also little things I learned—like, if you stick your chopsticks straight down into your rice, the Japanese superstition is that someone's going to die. I'd always do that as a kid, playing around, and my mom would get mad at me. And taking your shoes off in your house—all my shoes were at the door. And the furniture in the house—the paintings, dolls, and stuff that my parents bought in Japan—there was definitely a Japanese influence in that respect.

On holidays, like New Year's, we'd eat *mochi* [rice dumplings or patties] and sukiyaki [a Japanese dish]. And there was rice at every meal. My mother still cooks Japanese food daily. She'd cook another meal for my father—he grew up back east and prefers steak and potatoes. And so I'd eat both. I guess the dinner table was kind of a mixture of the cultures—Japanese culture and American, as well as African-American, the good old ribs and chicken and all that stereotypical stuff.

My dad loves music so I grew up with R&B and Motown and hip-hop and country and folk music. Don't limit yourself to just one style—that was a definite theme throughout my childhood. My parents obviously tried to steer us in the direction of being open-minded and accepting of other people and having a broad worldview.

I'm going to Japan. I'll be teaching English in this town between Osaka and Kyoto. I don't know how I'll be accepted there as a foreigner and being biracial. I'm sure in some circles I'll be looked down upon because of it. My mother feels the same way—that she would be discriminated against there because she married an African-American person.

I'm going to go there with an open mind. I'll travel as much as I can and enjoy the experience. I'm excited, I can't wait. My parents are more excited than I am. They know it's always been a dream of mine. And my family in Japan is just stoked about it.

I heard from Eric one year later. He was enjoying life in Japan so much that he decided to extend his stay another year. Here's what he said:

"I haven't had any problems living in Japan. I am obviously a foreigner, but I think being half Japanese has been a great advantage. The cultural transition was very easy. And many Japanese have pointed out that I act very Japanese and not like the typical *gaijin* [foreigner]. I take that as a compliment."

105

WE WANTED TO BE A NORMAL MCDONALD'S—EATING FAMILY

Stuart with his sister, Shannon.

STUART HAY, twenty
Fond du Lac, Wisconsin
Mother: Guyanese (West Indian)
Father: Canadian (Scottish, Irish, French)

I grew up in small-town Wisconsin. My mom didn't want to raise me and my sister in a place where there was going to be a lot of trouble. So my parents chose Wisconsin because Wisconsin seemed to be pretty peaceful.

You're very aware when you don't look like everybody else when you're a kid. Everybody else had two white parents. A lot of times we'd be someplace together as a family, like a restaurant or a store, and they'd ask, "Are you all together?" Or I'd be standing with my family, and they'd say, "Can I help you?" It was obvious that other people were not used to it.

We got along with the other kids okay, but it wasn't like we fit in, like we totally blended. I had problems, to a certain extent, with other kids when I wanted to enjoy my mother's ethnic foods or go places with her. I felt a little bit out of place or uncomfortable doing that. Sometimes it was easier to be seen with Dad because he's white and we were living in an all-white town. I kind of felt more eyes on me when I was with Mom. It was difficult.

106   When we had kids over to our house and my mom cooked for

us, they would turn up their noses. She might make curry or something. They wouldn't eat it or they would shove it over onto our plates. When we went over to their houses, their moms would make us pizza.

When you're little, you want to fit in and be normal—not different. When we were kids, we wanted to be a normal McDonald's-eating family. I tried to blend in with the white groups. I tried to deny a lot of my mom's culture, and I really didn't learn to appreciate her culture until I was older.

When we were in grade school, we had run-ins with some kids around the block. Their parents were racists and would teach their kids terrible things. They would say, "Is your mom from Africa?" We got called "nigger" and things like that. My parents were very caring and supportive. My mom and dad always taught us to be sorry for those ignorant people, and I think that helped to boost our self-esteem. The run-ins we had as kids strengthened us as individuals.

My parents did not bring up any controversy about the subject of race until we were old enough to handle it. All along we thought both sides of our family were very loving of each other. But once we were in high school, we found out that some people on my dad's side of the family had some prejudices about my mom. I think I had sensed it in a way. I just never felt as close to some people on my dad's side of the family as I did to people on my mom's side of the family.

My mom's family are just very warm, very beautiful people— and very caring. They live in Canada. We visit them a lot and I spend the summers with them. I found out from talking to them that we have mixed heritage all the way back to our great-grandparents. We have great-grandparents who were part British and part American Indian. And we have Chinese in there too. It's really interesting how this all came together. We're going to put a **107**

family tree together this summer to find out how many generations back we can go, to try to trace our roots from South America back to Africa.

*The homes of interracial families are often thought to be refuges
from racial intolerance and hatred. However, this is not always
the case. Racially mixed people who experience racism and prejudice in their own homes and families find it incredibly painful,
confusing, and infuriating.*

*Some young people witness parents blasting each other with
nasty racial comments. This sometimes occurs when a marriage
breaks up or in homes where anger spirals out of control.*

*Maria Root sees this as potentially hurtful to the kids, particu-
larly if they identify with the parent who is the target of the dis-
paraging comments. "It may hurt them tremendously because they
take it personally—they identify with that person. And it may drive
a wedge between that young person and the parent making those
comments."*

MY AUNT HAS A PROBLEM

JOY,* fourteen
Atlanta, Georgia
Mother: European-American
Father: African-American

On my dad's side, my aunt has a problem with the fact that my
dad married a white woman, and there's a little tension there. She
always acts sort of phony around me.

108   Just this past Christmas I was at my dad's family's house and they made a few comments against white people. I don't know why they were doing that—I was right there. When I came home, I was crying a lot because it hurt. I hope it doesn't happen again.

THEY ESSENTIALLY IGNORED ME

KARENA ACREE-PÁEZ, twenty-four
Alameda, California
Mother: Mexican-American
Father: European-American

I've never felt attracted to white men; I've always felt comfortable with Latino men. I've come to think that it has something to do with being very explicitly rejected by my father's family and then having my dad be absent and my mother as the only dominant figure in my upbringing.

When we would go to family gatherings, the rest of my cousins my age basically just didn't speak to me, and my grandmother would make very obvious gestures of favoritism toward my other cousins who weren't mixed. My sister and I looked very, very different from them. They're all of Irish or French descent so they all have blue or green eyes and either very, very blond or red hair. They essentially ignored me at these family things.

I remember my dad being very frustrated with my grandmother and my other relatives for manifestations of favoritism. For exam- **109** ple, when we were given Christmas gifts by my grandmother, she would buy very elaborate, beautiful gifts for my cousins, like dresses and things like that. And my sister and I would just get a coloring book or some crayons to share. It was very obvious.

After my parents were divorced I was still forced to go with my dad on Christmas and Thanksgiving. I never told my mother or my father how uncomfortable and miserable I was and how my other cousins treated me. A lot of times during Christmas or Thanksgiving dinners, I remember going into my aunt's bathroom to cry because I felt so horrible.

I stopped going to my father's family functions when I was about eleven.

"SO YOU HATE WHITE PEOPLE NOW?"

LAUREN,* eighteen
Mother: European-American
Father: Asian-American

My parents are in the process of getting a divorce right now. And I've noticed that recently my dad has made comments about white people, derogatory comments. He'll make these comments in front of my mom and it makes me wonder. It confuses me because my mom is white and he married her.

He's not directing it toward my mom necessarily, but toward whites in general, or people at work. But it still carries over to my mom because she's white. I'm half white, so it carries over to me.

110

And I'm just like, "Oh, okay, so you hate white people now?" It's like, "You're saying this, yet here I am, your child, and I identify with whites because that's what my mother is."

I know it's because they're in the process of a divorce and my mom is white and he's Asian and he's bashing her by making the comments. He's trying to hurt her and blame her for everything. And that's kind of strange, it's difficult.

ME AND MY DAD
CAN'T EVEN TALK

LAURENCE,* twenty-one
Mother: Asian-American
Father: European-American

When I was sixteen, I had an off day from school and me and one of my girlfriends were at my house. We were just hanging out. My dad came home from work and I guess he saw her shoes downstairs. So he came upstairs and he was like bang, bang, bang on my door. So I opened the door and he was like, "Who's in there?"

I said, "This is my friend Melanie." Melanie is black.

And he started yelling at her, "What the hell are you doing here?"

I'm like, "Dad, I invited her over, it's not her fault." And he was yelling at her, and I said, "Melanie, just go home, 'cause me and my dad are about to get into it."

So she went home and my dad said, "I don't want that nigger in the house!"

111

That was the first time I ever heard that word come out of his mouth. I lost a lot of respect for him. I didn't talk to him for a long time after that.

A couple months later I was getting my license and he was teaching me how to drive and he said, "Did you ever break up with that black girl?"

We had broken up. I knew that was what he wanted, so I said, "No, we didn't break up."

And he was like, "You're not getting your license until you break up with her."

It's real sad because he's always saying, "You get yourself a white girl or a Japanese girl." I laugh at that. I say, "I'm mixed race. How are you going to tell me that this girl ain't good enough because of the color of her skin?"

For my dad to have these views backed up by nothing—it's just completely hypocritical of him because he married an Asian. I'm like, "Look at our own family—we're not a Beaver Cleaver family."

There were a lot of other issues in my family. My dad's an abusive father. He would beat us pretty bad. I'm not saying I was a perfect kid growing up, but my dad has done some pretty ill stuff. I remember, when I was three or four years old, I stole a pack of gum. Well, he whooped me so bad, my back was bleeding.

When I was eight years old, my mom started taking karate lessons with us. So one day, when we were at the dinner table, she was playing around and she accidentally tapped his face. My dad picked her up by her neck and started choking her. She was hanging in the air and me and my brother and sister were sitting at the dinner table. Eventually he let her go and he walked out of the house and we didn't see him for a couple of days. It's things

112

like that that stick in your mind. I mean, my dad provided for us—we had food and we had our home—but I despised him.

I've talked to my grandma, my dad's mom, about it, because she's always trying to paint this pretty picture of our family. I said, "Where did Dad get all this? He's your son, he's my dad, but he needs some help."

My grandma thinks the same way my dad does about black and white relationships, but it doesn't affect me like my dad's views. My grandma says, "You need to get you a nice white girl with blue eyes and blond hair."

It makes me wonder what my dad's family thought about my mom, because my dad's father fought against the Japanese in World War II. From what he told my grandma, he killed a lot of Japanese. My grandparents eventually divorced because he was abusive and a real alcoholic.

My dad never spoke to his father after he left the house. But my grandma told my grandfather that he married a Japanese. I met my grandfather when I was nine years old. He said he wanted to meet my mom, but he didn't have a relationship with my father so he never met her. I went to his funeral and that was the second time I'd ever seen him in my whole life.

To this day, me and my dad can't even talk. There's such a big gap between our views. But I've come to the conclusion that I just have to be happy with myself. I used to always think, "Are my parents going to accept me if I do this?" It was too stressful. You've just got to do what makes you happy, even if that means being with somebody your parents don't approve of or making political statements that they don't agree with.

I want my own family to be better. The way I raise my kids—it's going to be totally different.

113

SHE DISMISSES A LOT OF RACISM

ELLEN,* twenty-two
Mother: Japanese-American
Father: European-American

Stereotypically, people think Japanese women are very timid and quiet—and that's just not the case. My mother is very strict and has very high expectations. She runs the house. She's very picky about who I date.

I feel that she looks at me as more culturally white because I think she sees me married to a white guy, and I know deep inside that I'm not gonna marry somebody white. I think she's always thought that I considered myself white. She doesn't understand what it's like to be biracial growing up in America, because she grew up in Japan.

She dismisses a lot of racism. I remember her arguing with the guy who used to fix her car. She said, "He can't understand me. He doesn't listen good enough." And I'm like, "Mom, maybe he's just being bigoted or racist." She wouldn't even consider that as a possibility.

My dad's much better. He always told me that I was special because I had the best of two different worlds and two different cultures. My dad was the one who really emphasized my being biracial. My dad is a really wise, wise old guy.

I think my mom's gotten much better about it. I think she's starting to realize that I'm different from her and that I don't consider myself white.

114

NO ONE GIVES ANY VALIDITY TO MY EXPERIENCES

LORI,* twenty
Mother: European-American
Father: Chinese-American

My family is very strange. My grandparents live two blocks away from me and I never see them. I wasn't ever too excited about seeing them because I always felt like a freak in my family because I'm so different and I am so much taller than everyone else. I was something they liked to look at and comment on, but I was never a part of the family.

They'd just look at me and say things about me in Chinese like, "Oh, she's so big." But they never made an effort to talk to me and they all know how to speak English perfectly well. I'd be in the corner with my brothers and my mom and we wouldn't have a clue what everyone was saying. We were just obviously so different.

When my parents were going to get married, my mom's parents were upset. My dad supposedly tried to convince them that he would take good care of my mom and that they really loved each other. I think my grandmother was okay with it then, but it was because she was enthralled with the idea of having these cute grandchildren who would look like China dolls. It freaks me out that she thought of me as such an object. But my grandfather was still very upset and didn't want the marriage to happen. He didn't want their children to have to suffer.

115

I think that growing up biracial is really rough. But that's because no one talked to me about it. Not to say that being biracial has ruined me, because I think that I'm a very confident person. But biracial, multiracial children have different issues that they need to deal with and I don't think my parents thought about those things too much.

My parents never talked to us about the fact that we were a biracial family, never. The first time we talked about it was two years ago because I brought it up. So not hearing about it from my family, not hearing about it through other people, I thought I was very alone.

My mom says that she didn't realize that I was having problems in school, which I found hard to believe because I remember coming home upset. I don't think she ever really questioned why. And many times I probably didn't talk about it because I was ashamed. If people at school called me names, I just didn't want to repeat it. And I didn't feel like it was something that anyone would understand if I tried to tell them about it.

Whenever my mom or dad knew something was happening to me that upset me because of my racial identity, their answer would always be, "You're special," or "You're beautiful, because you're biracial," and that didn't help me. That didn't help me understand why those kids were teasing me. My parents kind of brushed things off.

If there were a forum for me to talk about these things and understand these things, I would have been better off growing up. If my parents could have listened, I wish they could have even said, "If you ever have problems at school, please talk to us about it." My family isn't a very open one. If there's a problem, we just **116** don't talk about it.

I've taken a lot of classes that focus on Asian-American women, because that's the only way I can learn about my heritage. Last semester, I had a discussion with my mom and my brothers about what I was doing at school, and they just didn't understand why it was necessary for me to learn about the Chinese culture. I asked them how they didn't feel the same need. And then my brothers basically said that they consider themselves white. And then my mom said, "Yeah, I think of you kids as white," which was disturbing to me.

And then my brother said, "Yeah, and I think of Dad as white too." And that's when the *Twilight Zone* music started playing because my dad is not even close to being white—he's Asian. It taught me a lot about what my family thinks and what they want. They don't want to pay any attention to race. My mom always says that she doesn't understand why it's so important to me. There's a lot of denial going on.

I'd tell my mom that I walk down the street and people have literally grabbed my arm and stopped me and said, "So, what are you?" She doesn't want to believe that those things happen.

When I'm in Chinese restaurants with my dad, people always think that I'm not with him, we're not family. My dad and I went to this restaurant and there were two waiters who were talking in Chinese behind us. My dad told me later that they thought that he was a dirty old man and that we were going out together. My dad talked to them in Chinese and they were very embarrassed. My dad is always telling me, "Forget it, just brush it off." He tells me that these things shouldn't upset me, but they do.

No one listens to me; no one gives any validity to my experiences, not even my own father. I don't even know what I could say to make them understand what I'm feeling.

117

In her study of 200 interracial families, Maria Root found that the families "cover the whole spectrum from being very able and competent to talk about race to those families who avoid the issue because it's been really painful." Some parents avoid racial issues because they were rejected or ostracized by relatives for choosing an interracial relationship and family. "So they don't want to talk about it because it just hurts too much."

In other families, parents are simply unaware. They aren't mixed-race themselves, so they don't foresee the experiences and feelings that their multiracial children may have. Some white parents are racially naive, ignorant about the prejudice that people of color, including their mixed-race children, are subjected to. Parents who are people of color can also be naive in assuming that their children will not encounter racism because they have lighter skin or European-American features. "But there are all types of discrimination that a mixed-race person can experience."

Despite these problems, Root thinks young people who feel misunderstood by their parents shouldn't just write them off. "What I found in the study is that some of the kids just assume that their parents won't get it, so they won't talk to their parents. But when I talked to their parents, I found that they actually do get it and could be really helpful."

Parents don't have to be racially mixed themselves in order to be terrific parents to multiracial children. "Some parents have not had that experience, but they seem to be able to anticipate what their kids need and might experience." You'll read about a few of these families in the next few pages.

IN MY HOUSE, EVERY MONTH IS BLACK HISTORY MONTH

DEREK SALMOND, fifteen
Auburn, Washington
Mother: European-American
Father: African-American

I was born in Vallejo, California. We moved up here when I was about five or six. We're about fourteen miles south of Seattle. We have a fairly large percentage of different cultures here and so it's kinda cool—I'm not just seeing whites and blacks when I go to school. I think our school comes out to about 70 percent white, maybe 10 percent black, and then the rest are Asian and Pacific Islander and stuff like that.

Most people assume that I'm black. I always find that they're kind of surprised when they first meet my parents, or see them together, because they're black and white. And for the most part, no one's really had anything against it. I can only think of one problem that I've had. There was a girl on my water polo team. We had started going out and doing stuff together with groups of friends. She told her father about me and he just wasn't going to have it. He didn't want his daughter to hang out with someone of another ethnicity.

I was stunned at first, but I always knew it was going to happen eventually. It's something that both of my parents had prepared me for. They always made me aware that there is racism out there and that I was definitely going to stand out because I'm **119** of a different ethnicity. In many cases, it was just my dad telling me about encounters he had had. And when I started seeing girls, he reminded me that I was different and that girls may decide not to like me because of that, or that their parents may have problems with that. And that just made it easier for me to cope. When it came about, it wasn't as striking a blow for me as it may have been for others who wouldn't have been prepared for it.

I have parents who are willing to teach me what I don't learn in school. They encourage me and have the materials there and open to me. Some of the books we have are the *Black West* by William Katz and *Climbing Jacob's Ladder* by Andrew Billingsley. There's a book by Henry Louis Gates Jr.—*Colored People*. I know that I've read Ernest Gaines's *Lesson Before Dying*. I just read that again for the third time. One of the best movies I've ever seen is probably *A Raisin in the Sun*. My dad has a lot of videotapes from programs on TV—stuff about Thurgood Marshall and the Tuskegee Airmen and historical things.

At my house, I've always been encouraged to read black literature and to understand both sides of our culture. At home, it's more focused on the African-American side than on the Caucasian-American, because I learn so much about the Caucasian-American side in school. I think teachers are stunned that I know as much as I do. I've gotten into arguments in history class about issues that weren't correctly expressed in textbooks. Like when it came to the African slave trade, the book made it look like the Africans were uneducated people who wouldn't have survived on their own had the Europeans not come into their lives and provided for them.

It seems like the only time we learn about blacks in school is during February, which is Black History Month. In my house, **120** every month is Black History Month.

MY MOM CALLED US "HONEY BABIES"

Ayanna (far left) and her son, Frankie, are surrounded by her large extended family. Next to her are her stepfather, Randle Ross, and her mother, Sarah Ross.

OLAN MILLS

AYANNA MORIGUCHI, twenty-three
Eugene, Oregon
Mother: Seminole, Scottish, Irish
Father: African-American
Stepfather: African-American

Eugene has a small community of people of color. Everyone pretty much gets along. The majority of the black people in Eugene are mixed actually. There are a couple of families that are full black; both of the parents are black.

My mom helped found HONEY [Honor Our New Ethnic Youth] with some other mothers. It's a group for interracial families. It's mostly a social group—they have lots of picnics and potlucks. But they also talk about what their kids are going through. They requested that the school district have a multiracial category on school applications. And they got a park named after Martin Luther King Jr.

I was always involved in HONEY so I had a lot of biracial friends through it. I baby-sat during the meetings. I became a board member when I was about fourteen. I'm still involved. Right now I do Culture Club on Saturdays. Culture Club is a Saturday play group for kids to teach them about cultural diversity **121** and acceptance. We do art projects from different parts of the world. We talk about the lifestyles of the people where the project is from. My son is the youngest. Frankie is almost eleven months old.

Being interracial is one of the best parts of my life. It's been a plus. Having my mom be a part of HONEY has been really positive. I think it's made it easier for me. Like when my mom brought me to school, kids would say, "Are you adopted?"

And I'd say, "No, that's my mom."

And they said, "How come you're dark and she's white?" Having my mom tell me that being mixed is okay made it a really positive thing instead of something negative and confusing.

When you're a baby, you notice that your mom is white, your dad's black, and you're brown. My mom called us "honey babies," because our skin was the color of honey. That was how she explained it. As we got older, she would ask us how we felt about being mixed—like if we had any problems at school. And we were allowed to talk to her and tell her everything that was going on. If we were mad about it one day, then we could express that. She would accept it.

If we said, "You don't understand," she was like, "Yeah, I know I don't understand because I haven't lived what you're living." She never tried to tell us, "Yeah, I know what you're going through," because she didn't. She's white and we are mixed. She tried to empathize with us, but she would let us talk to her and tell her how we felt.

If we had to fill out forms and they said "Race, check one box," my mom always told us that we could leave that box empty because, if they were not going to make space for who we are, then we shouldn't have to fill it out. I'm mixed—I'm not black and I'm not white and I'm not Indian. I'm all three. My mom fought with the school district here and got that changed. Now you can mark "multiracial" as your race category. But I don't think you should ever have to mark down what your race is.

Parents should never try to make their kids choose one race or the other, but they should not try to stop them if they want to. My younger brother knows he's mixed. But to his friends he usually says he's black. So my mom's not going to say, "What about your white side?" He knows it's there. I think it's just that sometimes he feels like being black. It's probably easier for him in his situation.

Parents should definitely talk with their kids about not having to choose one race or the other. I think a lot of mixed people are confused about that—that you can be mixed and be proud and that nobody, not even your parents, can make you choose. That's important.

In the past twenty years, the parents of racially mixed children have come together and created dozens of groups like HONEY. Today there are between forty and fifty of these organizations across the country, from Berkeley, California, to Buffalo, New York, reports Ramona Douglass, president of the Association of MultiEthnic Americans (AMEA), an umbrella organization for many of them.

"These groups provide a structure in which dialogue feels safe and in which there's some sense of commonality and shared experience," she adds. Over potluck dinners and summer barbecues, parents exchange ideas and resources that enable them to be better parents. Their children have the opportunity to meet other mixed-race kids and see families that look like theirs. Racially mixed adults participate as well.

These groups also tackle larger issues. Some of them have successfully pressured school districts and state legislatures to rewrite **123** *racial identification questions to account for multiple heritages. According to Douglass, "They've created a grassroots political movement that has become the backbone for the multiracial movement."*

Most important, they played a role in the federal government's decision to change from "check one" to "check one or more" boxes in racial identification questions, despite initial opposition from larger and more powerful groups such as the National Association for the Advancement of Colored People. AMEA and other organizations representing multiracial community interests were in Washington, D.C., lobbying hard for this change.

"It was like a David and Goliath battle took place, and it's monumental that we're finally being acknowledged as not fitting into little rigid boxes anymore."

Although racial differences between mixed-race young people and their parents can cause profound misunderstanding and pain, race can also be a smokescreen for other issues and a weapon that rebellious teens use against their parents. "Kids know what buttons to push to drive their parents crazy," says Christine Iijima Hall, a psychologist who is herself Japanese and African-American. "And if they can add the 'race card,' that just freaks their parents out even more, especially if they have a white mother."

The first time I spoke to Maya, she and her mother were going through a bumpy period in their relationship. She thought the problem was that her mom was white. Months later, when I checked in with Maya again, she reported that their relationship was much improved. Looking back, she had some very wise obser-

124 *vations.*

RACE WAS A COVER-UP

MAYA COREY, nineteen
Minneapolis, Minnesota
Mother: European-American (German)
Father: African

One thing about biracial people is that their parents have to be strong, individualistic people. They don't have to do what everybody else is doing. For the most part, my mom doesn't care what other people think that much. She does what makes her feel right.

Lately there have been some issues we've talked about, especially with me going to college and the majority of my friends being black. She's a little bit offended and every so often she asks weird questions like, "Don't you talk to any white people? Don't you have any white friends? Have you ever liked white guys?"

For some reason lately, in arguments with her, I've made it racial, and for the most part, I really don't think it is. We'll argue and I'll say, "You wouldn't understand, you don't really get it."

It's really weird because for most of my life I felt she understood me. She told me that kids expect their parents to be perfect and all-knowing, but when you get to be a teenager and an adult you begin to realize that they're as human as you are. She said, "I think for a white person, I can understand about being biracial as well as anyone because I'm your parent."

I said, "You don't understand what it's like to be a minority." **125**

She said, "You know, you're right. I can try to sympathize or empathize as much as possible, but I never completely know because I'm not in your shoes." I think that's pretty much the truth of it. I never really believed it until now.

Your parents are the ones you're supposed to mirror, look up to, and want to become. And there is no way I can ever become my mother because she's white. In one very big way my mom is not like me. My skin is brown, so I'm going to experience life as a black person would. She can't understand that experience, which is so important in my life and affects my life so drastically.

She probably understands about being biracial as well as anyone possibly can because she raised a minority child and because of her closeness to me and her experiences with me, like being in a mall and experiencing racism. But at the same time it won't be complete. And that's the hard thing about the whole racial issue. People have to realize that they're not going to completely understand it and they have to try to empathize with the other side.

One and a Half Years Later . . .

I think race was a cover-up for other issues, maybe more on my part than my mom's. If I had issues with my mom, they were about other things—personality, monetary issues, whatever. I always knew my mom was my mom and I didn't really care what race she was. But I knew that race was a sensitive area for her.

Being a single mom, she's given so much of herself to me. For eighteen years she did everything. That's been difficult for her, and she should be commended because I think she did a wonderful job. She gave me a lot of things—emotional and financial [security], et cetera. I was in a lot of extracurricular activities. I went to a private school. I had material things that I wanted. She even made breakfast every morning for me. I think she liked to do all that. But she didn't feel appreciated. She could get very, very upset and unhappy. And I was a difficult child. I knew that, no matter how far I pushed her, eventually I'd get what I wanted, and I'd push and push her.

When I spoke to you, I'd just finished my first year at Duke, which is a really expensive school. I know Duke is the ideal place for me and offers a lot of opportunities. But at that point, my mom was questioning why she should give more of herself, why she should give up so much for me. And that made me upset and a little confused. I thought, "How could she do this all along, and then now, when it really counts, consider taking it all away?" And so we'd argue, and be so impassioned and yell, and we'd both hurt each other and say horrible things.

It's better now. I've matured and I don't expect as much of her anymore. She deserves to do for herself. I really would like to take some of the burden off of her and graduate and make some money and become a little bit more independent. I owe her a lot for everything she's done.

I WASN'T THE BLUE-EYED, BLOND-HAIRED CHEERLEADER TYPE

LISA, eighteen
Northern New Jersey
Mother: Chinese-American
Father: European-American (English)

My dad is always saying, "When I was your age, I went on my vacation. I wanted to see the world. And I think that was a good move." My dad grew up in England. In breaking away and marrying my mom, he was doing something very rash.

My dad went to Taiwan and I think my parents met over the summer. From what their longtime family friends say, it was a very romantic courtship involving my dad being relentlessly dogged and determined to somehow marry my mother. She got a scholarship to an American school, and basically he followed.

I feel lucky to be half Asian and half English. If anything, it's taught me from a very early age to be very open-minded. I feel like there's a lot of diversity within my own house. We'll have the Christmas tree up and then we'll have the little Buddhist statues. And we have books on the shelf in Chinese and English. I speak Mandarin.

My town is an upper-middle-class town in New Jersey. It's a quaint town. The main streets are lined with antique shops and you can get all the patchwork quilts you ever dreamed of there. Once we were sitting in English class and someone described my town as a Ziploc bag—nothing new came in and nothing new came out. In terms of race, there's not that much diversity. There are not a lot of African-Americans, not a lot of Asian-Americans.

A lot of the time, I think it's hard for people to tell that I'm related to my family. I'm five foot ten inches and my mom is five foot sixish. And my dad is this pale Englishman. I don't look too much like either of them individually. But if you see my father next to my mother, you can kind of see where my height would come in, and my face.

And to this day, my dad is always wary of walking with me in public. He says, "Lisa, you're older now. People are going to think I'm like Woody Allen." He always says, "When you're around me, please address me as 'Daddy' a lot." I don't think he wants people to get the wrong impression.

In elementary school, I remember kids making fun of the differences by calling me "Chink," and just being really racist. A lot of it was little kids not knowing what they were doing. But I felt very persecuted, especially when I was that young. Like, what did I do to provoke something like that—just being born a combination of these nationalities? At times like that I just wanted to go home and turn invisible.

If you were Asian, they assumed you were a nerd or that you were socially introverted. It was the Madonna "Material Girl" phase, where everybody was wearing socks rolled up and teased blond hair. And here I was, this very Asian-looking girl with very straight hair, bangs cut just so, wearing very conservative British-type school uniforms. There was a standard for popularity and beauty that I just didn't fit into at that time—you know, the blue-eyed, blond-haired cheerleader type.

So I just wanted to change—I wanted plastic surgery, I wanted to dye my hair, I wanted blue eyes. And I didn't want to be the studious girl who sat in the front row and played piano after school. I wanted to be cool. I wanted to be popular and hip. And I was so depressed that I wasn't.

I was ashamed to admit any of my insecurities to my parents, because, in reality, I was ashamed of who I was. I didn't want to tell my parents, "I don't like what you guys created—me." By not having faith in myself, it seemed like I somehow did not have faith in them or in the choices they had made, because I was the product of those choices.

It took my grandmother, as an outsider, to see what was going on. She's a very perceptive woman and a very loving woman and I felt safe confiding in her. My grandmother had doubted my parents' marriage at first. When my mom and my dad decided to get married, there was definitely a lot of opposition from my mom's family. My father, as a white man in Taiwan, was very much looked down upon. And his marriage to my mom, who lived in a relatively well established and pretty high-up family, was a big scandal. I think they opposed the marriage because they worried about what kind of a future their daughter would have and not necessarily from an anti-Caucasian feeling.

But now my grandmother loves my father arguably more than she loves any of her other family members. She didn't want people to judge me wrongly as she had once judged my father. My grandmother had a talk with me and it was very influential. She told me that I had the elements to be everything I wanted to be, but that first I would have to learn to be myself. She helped me realize that I had a lot to be proud of and that I didn't have to fit in with everybody else.

At my high school, I was the same person essentially. Except now I went in with a complete acceptance of myself. I just projected a more confident image. I was a lot more secure with who I was. In turn, I think once people saw that I was not ashamed of who I was they also become a lot more accepting.

I think when people judge you and persecute you because of something like race it stems from definite insecurities on the part of the persecutors. And when I look back now, I see a bunch of little kids who were trying to prove something, trying to fit in, and the easiest way for them to do that was to find a common thing to make fun of.

There's always the bully who makes himself feel like he has self-worth by bullying other kids. I think these bullies are to be pitied as much as or even more than the people they attack. Because when people are attacked, it can either weaken them or make them stronger. They can either want to conform or they can realize that they don't want to conform to a system that breeds people like that. So I think it can be a definite learning experience.

My family was very supportive just by the example they set. Here's a Caucasian man and an Asian woman, married. And sure, they have differences. I definitely would say there was a lot of turmoil and a lot of times when they could have said, "Is it worth it?" because of all the pressure that they received.

But still I saw that they loved each other. And I thought, "What kind of an environment do I prize more—the one I see here at home or the one where a bunch of kids are bored after school and have nothing better to do than to take it out on other people?" You need a lot of spirit and a lot of strength and passion to persevere in the face of that much social and cultural opposition. And I think seeing my parents do that has made me a bit pigheaded, but also very determined to fulfill my own dreams.

STICKS AND STONES

"Being biracial, you get the best of both worlds, but you also get the worst," says sixteen-year-old Amanda Holzhauer. Amanda, whose mother is African-American and whose father is white, says the worst is experiencing prejudice from both sides—from racist whites because she is black and from prejudiced blacks because she is white.

In a society fragmented by racial tensions and divisions, biracial and multiracial people are often caught in the crossfire of hatred and mistrust between different groups.

"SORRY, TRY AGAIN"

KURTIS FUJITA, twenty
Agoura Hills, California
Mother: European-American (Irish, English)
Father: Japanese-American (Hawaiian)
Stepfather: European-American

When I was growing up, no one could tell what I was, so I would get discriminated against, but always for being the wrong race. A lot of people thought I was a Mexican or Persian. If people were hassling me, they usually used a Mexican racial slur, like "beaner." I got called every type of slur but what was correct. I'd be like, "Sorry, try again. Go down the list until you get it right."

It was annoying at first and I would be offended. But in a way, **134** it was kind of funny, because people were really off. It gave me empathy for people in other racial groups, because I was getting discriminated against because people thought I was one of them. I have more empathy for anyone who has been discriminated against because of the fact that I'm mixed.

IT'S NOT EVEN ABOUT BEING MIXED

ERNEST WHITE II, eighteen
Jacksonville, Florida
Mother: French-Canadian, Black
Father: African-American

My junior year in high school, I was a foreign-exchange student in Sweden. I spent my last week in Stockholm. A lot of American tourists were there. A guy was standing in front of me going up the escalator out of the subway. I knew he was American. He turned around and looked at me and then patted his wallet to make sure it was still there. I got .38 hot. I was like—I can't even get away from it in Sweden.

I went into a store in Tallahassee to buy a computer and even the black salesman ignored me and went to help the white young females from Florida State who were probably buying a video camera half the price of a computer. I was in there to spend money, but it took me forty-five minutes to get help. What did I have to do—slam a computer against the wall?

135

All black folks have experiences like that—that's just a given. If you're black, you're going to be looked at funny; you're going to be ignored. Like, if I walked into a car showroom and said I wanted to go on a test drive, they're not going to let me do it, even if I had the money. But if Winthrop Oglethorp III came in, they'd probably let him sign a lease right then. So it's not even about being mixed. If you're dark, you're going to get discriminated against—period. Being black is hard.

THERE'S ALWAYS A SECURITY GUARD AROUND

MIRIAM WARREN, sixteen
Las Vegas, Nevada
Mother: European-American (German)
Biological Father: Filipino-American
Adoptive Father: European-American

If I go into an upscale department store and I just happen to be with my boyfriend, who is African-American, security guards follow us everywhere. I know this stuff does not happen when I'm with my white friends.

Instead of getting mad about this, and being quiet and mad, I say, "Hey, isn't this funny! Every time we come to the store and there's a black person in the store wanting to buy something, there's always a security guard around. Why is that?" I'll say it loud, because they should be exposed for that. It's completely stupid, because criminals come in all different colors, not just one.

When you are faced with racial injustice, you can get really mad and go out and do something really bad. Or you can do stuff that embarrasses the person who's creating the racial injustice. It's only when people start talking about it, and saying it loud, that other people will start to hear.

Some people just need to be knocked in the head and yelled at a couple of times for them to realize that their behavior is unacceptable. They are going to have to change their views, or they'll have to crawl into a hole or something, because the rest of the world is progressing and they are going to get left behind.

I HAVE TO PROVE MYSELF

BRIAN HARRIS, sixteen
Stanton, California
Mother: European-American
Father: African-American

I think there's still racism everywhere. It's not as outwardly noticeable as it once was; there are not as many crosses burning in people's yards. But it's still there—a lot of it is institutionalized. I think there are still a lot of stereotypes and that people are not given a fair shot at things when they are assumed to be less qualified because of their race.

Sometimes there are teachers who assume that I'm not going to be as intelligent as their white students are. If I go up and ask them a question, they'll be a little put out. They'll be like, "Didn't I already go over that? Can't you listen?"

Why do they have an attitude? It's their job to help you out. After a while, they realize that I'm on the same level as the other **137** students—I'm getting the same grades or better. But I have to prove myself first.

I try not to overreact. Some people get overly sensitive about things. Like they might be walking through a mall and someone looks at them and they think it's because of their race, because they're biracial. But it might be because the person likes their shirt or something. If I go through the same mall and someone looks at me, I'll probably go, "Hey, maybe they think they know me." So I don't assume that every reaction I get from other people is because of my race.

For the most part, teachers have been fine, great people, and just a few of them have given me an attitude. But sometimes I'll look back later and realize, "That was a little odd—they'd rather ask a question to one of the other students and pretend like I'm not here."

I WAS MADE TO FEEL THAT I WAS INFERIOR

KARENA ACREE-PÁEZ, twenty-four
Alameda, California
Mother: Mexican-American
Father: European-American

I was the only Chicana in my elementary school and one of two or three in middle school and high school. I would often get questions from other students. They would say, "What are you? Italian? Are you Greek?" I would just mention that my dad was

Irish and French. I was embarrassed to mention that my mother was Mexican, and if I could avoid mentioning it, I did.

Sometimes I mispronounced English words and other children teased me. The person who taught me English was my mother and she taught me the words in her accented speech. When I had fights with my school friends, I was called "spic" or "beaner." The words were a weapon. They were very openly spoken.

In California, you can imagine how many derogatory terms there are for immigrants newly arrived from Mexico and Latin America. That stereotype of a wetback was associated with any Latino or Spanish-speaking person. And so I just absorbed all those ideas and it became something I was definitely embarrassed about, something that I felt I would be inherently associated with.

People associate a class with each ethnic group. When they hear you speaking Spanish, which I do all the time now with my husband and my family, they assume that you're some migrant worker or something. When I was very young, I made the association that Mexicans were from lower-income areas, and that contributed to my identification of being Mexican as something bad. I had very, very low self-esteem.

That first year I was away from Alameda, when I had gone to Columbia University and was living in New York, I had a chance to disassociate myself from all those feelings of self-hatred. I was able to piece together an identity that I feel comfortable with. I feel comfortable in saying that I'm Chicana.

But I feel really resentful toward the white community sometimes for making me feel that I was inferior, or that I could never be pretty because I wasn't fair-skinned. I was essentially made to feel like I should deny my mother, who has been everything to **139** me. I was made to feel inferior because being Chicana was part of me, when it's actually the strongest part of me and something that I'm now very proud of.

Multiracial people find prejudice on both sides of the fence—from people of color as well as from whites.

IT SAID "OREO," THEN IT SAID "YOU"

KEVIN MAILLARD, twenty-four
Tulsa, Oklahoma
Mother: Black Indian
Father: African-American

There were black people at Duke [University] who came from the suburbs but once they got to Duke they automatically switched to, like, "Oh, I grew up in this housing project." People who'd never listened to rap music in their lives suddenly became Tupac Shakur's biggest fans. They'd buy different clothes and talk differently. People who went to boarding schools would be like, "Yo." It was absolutely ridiculous. It happens at all of these private schools—people are always trying to prove themselves as "authentically black," and I just did not feel comfortable with that because that's not me.

The harshest comments I've gotten have come from other black people. When black people pass by me, they'll imitate my accent. So a lot of times when I'm passing other black people at the mall or just walking along, I shut up.

140

My freshman year at Duke I was watching a movie with my friend and someone slipped a letter under my door. We opened the letter and there were all these Ebonic terms in it. It said "Oreo," then it said "YOU." It said "Lame . . . YOU." "Real" and underlined in red "NOT YOU." And then it said "Step Off . . . you need to read this 'cause you don't know anything."

I was really annoyed, because, first of all, it interrupted our movie and it was a good movie. The guy who did it lived down the hall from me. I didn't even know him. So I wrote this letter to the school newspaper, because I wanted to embarrass him and I wanted people to know that this stuff goes on.

I wrote that black people had worked so long to overcome prejudice and isn't the meaning of prejudice to prejudge someone? And who are these people to decide who would be considered black and what would be authentic or not authentic, because from my perspective maybe they are not what I consider to be black.

After the newspaper came out, there were black people walking around giving me the evil eye. They were angry with me for exposing intraracial prejudice.

The guy who wrote the letter went on to become head of our black student organization.

THERE WAS ALWAYS HARASSMENT

STEVE PHILLIPS, sixteen
St. Louis, Missouri
Mother: European-American
Father: African-American

I used to go to this school. It was bad there. There was too much stuff going on—violence, drugs, and stuff I wouldn't mess with. There was always harassment. People put people down all the time. It was all black; the ones who were different got picked on.

I was different mostly because of my hand and my being biracial. My hand is kind of messed up; the bones didn't grow right. So they'd say things. They liked to call me "cripple." They would say, "You white bastard" or "Oreo." That was an everyday thing there. I didn't tell anyone about it. You do that there, and you'd have to watch your back for the rest of the year.

But most of what they'd say would go in one ear and out the other. I didn't care what they said as long as they didn't lay a hand on me. If someone throws a punch at me, I'm going to throw one back.

All the harassment got in the way of my studies. It was too **142** much. I had to get away from it. I heard that I could get into the technical school. I got accepted and I went there the following year.

I was at the technical school a whole month and then I got into a fight on the bus 'cause a guy twice my size just kept harassing me. He was one of the ones who harassed me all the time last year. He used to harass me in middle school too.

I was sitting at the front of the bus and he was all the way in the back. He was saying ignorant stuff about my race. I just let it go in one ear and out the other. But finally, I had enough. He threw a book and hit me in the back of the head and I got up and punched him in the face. I'm not ashamed to say that he really overpowered me. He had me up against the window. Some kids pulled me off him, but I ran back. That was stupid, but once I get going, I get going.

After the police got there, they told me to get off the bus. Another cop came, shoved me to the ground, put his knees in my back, and cuffed me up. They took me to the police station and had my mom come and get me.

I'm not at school now. They acted like they didn't want me there because of the fight. I wanted to work. So when a job opened up, I took it. I have a full-time job now. I work at Dairy Queen. I'll just get my GED and go to a community college.

"The Asian-American communities, and Asia as well, are infamous for their belief in racial purity and for not being accepting of mixed-race people." Cindy Nakashima, who is Hapa, came to this insight from writing about mixed-race people and teaching a class on the subject at the University of California at Berkeley. Racially mixed people who have an Asian heritage do not necessarily feel the need to connect with Asian-Americans or to be accepted by **143**

them. However, those who find it meaningful to embrace their Asian heritage often find that they are not embraced back, adds Nakashima. "Mixed-race people talk about feeling like they have to prove themselves. It can be pretty frustrating and it can be painful."

Nakashima attributes some of the Asian-American intolerance to a history of wars fought in Asia and the American military presence there. As a result, hundreds of thousands of mixed-race children were born—many out of wedlock—to American GIs and Asian women. Illicit sex, illegitimacy, and interracial relationships are linked in the minds of many Asians and some Asian-Americans. Mixed-race people, particularly those who are Asian and black, are stigmatized.

The Japanese-American community is now beginning to broaden the definition of Japanese-American because more than half of Japanese-Americans marry non-Japanese; practically every family has racially mixed members. "And Hapas are getting really vocal about being excluded," Nakashima observes. The group Hapa Issues Forum, for example, was started by mixed-race young people to pry open the Japanese-American community, and they've achieved a lot of success.

Filipino-Americans are generally more accepting of racially mixed people, notes Nakashima, because racial mixing has been more common in the Philippines, a former colony of Spain. In the Philippines, there is actually a sort of reverse prejudice whereby looking white or having white heritage is valued.

HATE CRIME IN JAPANTOWN

ROCKY KIYOSHI MITARAI, twenty-one
Sonoma, California
Mother: European-American
Father: Japanese-American

I was raised in Sonoma, California, which is a small, predominantly Caucasian town. When I was growing up, people made slanted eyes in front of me and called me names. Since I was fat, they asked me if I was going to be a sumo wrestler. I kind of accepted it and made fun of myself too, so that I would fit in.

Once, when I was in seventh grade, we were told by the music teacher to get into groups and make songs. This other group put up a big piece of butcher paper, and on it was a picture of a man with a rice picker's hat, buckteeth, and two slanted lines for eyes. Their song didn't involve much more than these lines: "I come from China. I don't care if you kill me. I eat sushi. And my eyes are so slanted that I can't see."

After they were done, all the kids in the class were laughing. Even the teacher was laughing. I felt angry, but I didn't know why. I had been hearing racist things throughout my life and I had started to feel as if it were normal. My friends who wrote the song said, "Why is that song racist? It's not even racist." They continued to sing the song for the rest of the year and made other jokes about Asian people.

145

After I was out of school for the summer, I was talking with my dad and I told him about the song. He was furious and wanted to get the teacher fired.

In the eighth grade, I hung out with a kid who was half African-American and half Caucasian and another kid who was Cuban-American. There were hicks—cowboy types—who would scream obscenities at us, like "You f—ing Mexicans," for example. If you were a person of color and hung around other people of color, it was automatically assumed that you were a gangster, wanna-be gangster, or that you wanted to be black.

Things like that hurt me while I was growing up, which is probably why I denied my Caucasian side after grammar school and identified myself as full Japanese.

My father told me many stories about my Japanese ancestry and how important it is. He told me that our family is of the samurai class—warriors who lived by a strict code of honor, and would go as far as death to uphold this code. My *jichan* [grandfather] would always remind my father that we need to be proud of and show respect to our ancestors. My *jichan* was a very honorable man. He was raised with Japanese cultural values. One's family, job, friend, or obligation comes before an individual's wants in Japan.

What happened in 1942 changed my *jichan*'s life, along with the lives of all people of Japanese ancestry in America. During World War II, President Roosevelt signed Executive Order 9066, which authorized the evacuation of everyone on the West Coast who was seen as a threat to the war effort. Thus all the Japanese-Americans were interned. My father, at the age of three, and his family were sent to the Heart Mountain Relocation Center in Wyoming. They were given ten days' notice to sell everything

they owned.

The relocation camps were located on very barren, desertlike land. It was terribly cold in the winter, especially in the small crowded wooden shacks that every family had. The bathrooms there were just big rooms with toilets, usually without partitions around them.

When my family finally got out in 1945, there was no house or land to go back to. They had had a successful farming business before the war, which they also lost. My *jichan* did his best to start over from nothing and support the family. He began to farm strawberries, and had to work hard to make ends meet.

When my father was in school, he did his homework and then went out to the strawberry fields. He has marks on his knees now from squatting down to pick and plant strawberries so much in his early life. My father doesn't think my *jichan* ever recovered from the whole terrible thing. At the age of eighty-five, after living a hard life, he passed away.

When I think about things like this, I feel enraged. But at the same time, I have such admiration and pride for my family and my people for standing strong through all of this oppression and allowing me to live the good life that I do now.

I thought it would be great to go to a school where whites were not the majority. I came to the University of San Francisco so I could be with other Asians because I felt that they were the ones who would support me. But when I finally got to USF, my world seemed to collapse around me. The Asians here usually hang out together in big cliques—cliques that I couldn't be a part of. I am not accepted by many as an "Asian" person. I hear things from people like: "Why do you try so hard to be full Japanese?" "Why is your last name Japanese?" "You shouldn't be in the Japan Club—you aren't a real Japanese." "Eating rice today, huh? Are you getting in touch with your Asian side?" "Hey, what's up, Mexican? What's up, Paco? Do you want to eat some refried beans?" "Look at this guy—the Asians don't want him, the Caucasians don't want him. He might as well be a Mexican."

I am often criticized for doing "Japanese" things, such as eating with chopsticks, practicing martial arts, or even making a simple trip to Japantown. People ask me why I do these things and some people even tell me that I shouldn't do them. I was raised doing them, and now that I have grown up and people can't see my Asian physical characteristics, I am criticized about the way I live.

One recent experience taught me some very hard lessons about the world. On Friday, May 9, 1997, I was attacked and nearly killed by a group of Asians because I am Hapa. That night, I went to sing karaoke in San Francisco's Japantown with four of my friends. When we were leaving for the night, there were about ten Chinese and Vietnamese guys standing outside of the karaoke studio. As a good luck charm, I wear a Chinese character on my necklace that says *fuku,* meaning "happiness" in Japanese and "good fortune" in Chinese. They were all staring at me angrily and I heard one of them say, "But why is he wearing that necklace? He doesn't even know what it means."

I knew that they had a problem with me because I am not "full" Asian. My friends told them that I am half Japanese, but that didn't seem to matter.

I left the building and started walking to my car. I turned around and saw three of them walking behind me. They all started punching me in the face and stomach. Then one of them began choking me. I fell down, and they started kicking me in the head. At this point, I was covering my head trying to protect myself, and thinking that I might die. My friends did not help me. I guess they were too scared to act.

I got up and then the same three guys came after me and beat me some more. One of the guys yelled, "You see Bruce Lee movies and you want to be Asian, huh?!"

I kept telling him that I was half Japanese. Finally, he left with all of his friends. My necklace had been ripped off. My friend found it for me. It was bent and broken.

I must have been struck in the face and head at least thirty-five times. I had huge bruises on the side and back of my head, a black eye that I couldn't see out of, and a swollen head for about a week. These physical injuries have healed now, but the mental scars will not go away so fast.

Things have gotten to the point where I am almost killed by other Asians because of my way of life. I can't just *stop* being Japanese. I have worn that necklace for many years and it reflects who I am, and that I am proud of being Japanese. I have just as much right to wear it as anybody else.

After my violent experience in Japantown, it became clear to me that something must be done to stop the oppression that Hapa people face every day. I wrote an e-mail describing my assault to Hapa Issues Forum, which is a Hapa club at U.C. Berkeley. I got a great deal of support from them. An article about my experiences as a Hapa person was printed in the *Pacific Citizen*, a Japanese-American newspaper, and I was interviewed by a man from the *Nichi Bei Times*, another Japanese-American newspaper. He is trying to create a column in the paper to regularly address Hapa issues.

Identifying myself as Hapa is very important to me. I do have an identity. I shouldn't just be seen as some confused person who doesn't fit in anywhere. I want people to understand that being multiethnic—half Japanese and half Caucasian, for example— **149** does not mean that you only know half of your culture. People can't assume that culturally we are any less Asian or Pacific Islander than anyone else. A person can't be split down the middle.

Many Hapa people's experiences today are similar to those of the Japanese-Americans about thirty years ago. Many of them had an identity crisis because their knowledge of Japanese language and culture was limited because their parents tried to mold them into "Americans" for their own good and protection. At the same time, people were constantly questioning their knowledge about the United States and their ability to speak English. They were judged by their appearance and nothing else. I know that the oppression I have been subject to is not at all equal to what my father and Japanese family went through during the terrible internment experience. But the rejection, the necessity to prove my "Asianness," and being hated because of my multiethnic background are things that weigh heavily on my mind every day.

People may choose not to accept who I am because I am Hapa, but this ignorance cannot change me. Nobody can take my heart and spirit away from me. I am a very proud Japanese-American.

A portion of this story was originally published in What's Hapa'ning: The Hapa Issues Forum Newsletter.

Even though the U.S. Supreme Court struck down laws forbidding interracial marriage in 1967, many people, both white and non-white, are strongly opposed to it. Organized hate groups such as the Ku Klux Klan and neo-Nazi skinheads, as well as black separatist groups such as the Nation of Islam, routinely denounce interracial couples or "race mixers." Each year hate-crime statistics include incidents of harassment, intimidation, and assault against interracial couples, families, and individuals.

The prejudice against interracial sex and marriage runs deep in ordinary Americans as well. This aversion is reflected in some of the vocabulary used to describe mixed-race people—mutt, half-breed, mongrel. *These derogatory terms imply that love and sex between people of different races is unnatural, even animalistic.*

After I finished writing this book, an eighteen-year-old girl in Houston, Texas, told me about an ugly experience that opened her eyes to the irrational hatred some people have for those who are racially mixed. Monica, whose mother is white and whose father is African-American, was surfing the net when she encountered a young man in a chat room. "He said, 'I've always hated black people, but you're worse than black—you're mixed, you're like a mutt. When dogs are mixed, they're not as valuable or intelligent as pure breeds—and that's what happens when you mix races, you get the worst out of both.' He said I was a weaker person because I was mixed, and that everything—my health, my intelligence, and my looks—was second rate because I wasn't one race or the other. I knew that there wasn't any truth to it. I was really mad. I was arguing with him. But you can't change somebody's views."

The belief, held by some ignorant and bigoted people, that racially mixed people are genetically inferior to others has absolutely no scientific validity.

"PURINA DOG CHOW" AND "CHOW MEIN"

JENNIFER CHAU, twenty
Queens, New York
Mother: Jewish European-American
Father: Chinese-American

My mother is Jewish and my dad is an atheist. Both of my parents wanted to raise me and my brothers as Jews. So I started Hebrew school at the age of six or seven. In Hebrew school, you study the culture and traditions of Judaism. But for the most part, you learn how to read Hebrew and you have no clue what you're reading.

We were the only family there that was biracial. Everybody else had two Jewish parents. I only had one, and then, my dad was also Chinese. So a lot of people in my class would torment me because I was the only different one. They would make fun of my last name because everybody else's was "Bernstein," or something like that. My last name is Chau, and I remember kids in both regular school and Hebrew school always calling me "Purina Dog Chow" and "chow mein" and stuff like that.

I hated my last name so much. When I was little, I wanted to get rid of it because it was the main indicator to people that I was different. Everyone gets made fun of at school, but I was always made fun of for my last name or the fact that my dad was Chinese. It was always racial.

The teachers were nice to me but I remember the rabbi being very discriminatory. There were very little things, but I knew that

152

those things were happening to me because I was different. Once we were walking into the little synagogue; my whole class was there and I just happened to be the last one in line. The rabbi held the door open for everyone, and as soon as I got there, he stepped in front of me, went in, and let the door slam in my face. It wasn't like I was a little thing that he could just overlook; I was as tall as he was. I felt like those kinds of things were happening to me because I was biracial.

It was so frustrating, because they should have considered me as much of a Jew as anyone else there. By Jewish law you are Jewish if your mother is Jewish, and my mom is Jewish. But I was always treated as a lesser person. I have two younger brothers and they had a lot of problems there, too, with kids in their classes making fun of them. And there was one boy who was in my brother's class—he was black, adopted by a Jewish woman— who got the same sort of teasing and tormenting. It was just not a place where you could be different; you really had to fit in.

The worst thing happened when it was time for my bat mitz-vah [a coming-of-age ceremony]. I was twelve. Bar (for boys) and bat (for girls) mitzvahs are huge deals for many people, especially the girls in my Hebrew class. You prepare for it for what feels like a year—reserving the space for the party, picking out the food, ordering the invitations, figuring out the guest list, getting the dec-orations and the DJ, and finding a photographer to do a profes-sional video of the whole event. There were at least a hundred people at my reception and it was considered a small one.

A bat mitzvah is always on Saturday during the regular service. There would be hundreds of people there—the regular congre-gation and everyone I invited, including all of my friends.

So on Thursday we had the rehearsal with the cantor and everything was fine. Then Friday night the head of the ritual com- **153** mittee called my mother and said that they had just had a special meeting and decided that my father could not take part in the ceremony because my being up there with both of my parents would mean the synagogue promoted intermarriage and they didn't want to promote intermarriage.

My mom was hysterical. My father wasn't very surprised. He didn't feel welcome there. I was upset, but I didn't really understand how horrible it was. I just knew that they didn't like my dad because he was Chinese. And it affected me the whole day of the ceremony—it was basically ruined.

They told my mom that she could still go up on the altar with me. But she didn't want to go up without my father. If only one parent goes up there with the child, it looks like the other parent is dead. So my grandparents came up with me. I was the only kid in my class who didn't have her parents up there, and from that day on, I didn't want to have anything to do with my Jewish heritage. I still think it's very important to me, but I can't tell you what I learned in Hebrew school because I threw it all out when that happened.

I had known these people since I was six years old. I went to the school three times a week, two hours each time. Although I always felt like they treated me a little worse than the other kids, I still felt like they were some sort of support system for me because I had known them for such a long time. And then, on the day that I had worked for the whole time I was in Hebrew school, they basically stabbed me in the back.

A couple of years later, I started to understand what had happened, and I became really, really angry. I wanted to confront the rabbi about what he had done. I wanted to tell him off. I remember thinking about it at least once a day, every single day. It tormented me. It was an unresolved piece of my life.

I didn't want to go back then because my brothers were still there. I didn't want my brothers to suffer for anything that I did. And that was supposedly the most open synagogue in our area, so there wasn't really anywhere else for them to go that would have been better. So I waited.

Then, last summer, I scheduled an appointment with the rabbi. I thought I was going to be very rough and tough, but I just started bawling as soon as I started talking. I was still very, very, very upset about the whole situation. I think he felt bad because he saw how much I was still hurting after eight years.

He denied everything I said about discrimination in the synagogue. But he did say that they should have handled the bat mitzvah differently. He said that non-Jews are not allowed to go up on the altar. He said that was policy, but that they should have told us that when we came to the synagogue when I was six, because it's assumed when you join a Hebrew school that you are going to be bat mitzvahed there.

The rabbi was apologetic. I thought that was a great thing because they showed no remorse around the time of my bat mitzvah. They were really hurtful and they didn't acknowledge it in any way. So I felt like it was very resolved after that. I felt like a weight was lifted.

And then my mom told me that someone who was on the ritual committee told her that the rabbi came in to one of their meetings and said, "There is this girl who came to talk to me this summer who was very courageous. She told me about a situation that happened to her here and she wanted to have it resolved." He said that they needed to inform new people so that this didn't happen again.

I was excited that this happened. My time there was very hard because everyone noticed that I was different and made me feel **155** bad about it. But at least some things have changed—if anyone like me comes along in the future, they'll be aware of the policy.

But I'm still disgusted by the fact that a family member would be excluded because he is not Jewish. That is why I will never force Judaism on my children. It did not welcome me at all. There was no place for me in my synagogue.

Not all synagogues exclude a non-Jewish or nonreligious parent from participating in a child's bar mitzvah or bat mitzvah. These policies differ from congregation to congregation and reflect the wide spectrum of opinion on issues of interfaith marriage among American Jews.

Although the numbers are contested, recent surveys show that between 38 and 52 percent of American Jews marry non-Jews. While more traditional Jews often see intermarriage as a threat, those who are more secular or assimilated tend not to feel they have to choose between their religion and their love for a person of any background.

This concern—that marriage to outsiders leads to cultural extinction—has been raised in other communities, such as the Japanese-American and Native American, where the outmarriage rates are also especially high.

Are these fears justified? Is the assumption that racially mixed young people are quick to turn their backs on their cultural heritages valid? Not according to what I've found. Admittedly, my research was not based on a carefully constructed survey, but the majority of the multiracial people I talked to were engaged in some sort of cultural exploration. They were studying in Beijing, learning how to speak Japanese, participating in Native American rituals, and writing research papers about their family

REFLECT

I walk to [the mirror] and look in

to the outside of me.
my face usually belongs to
others
but now it's
mine.
my eyes squint as I try
to pretend that I'm someone else—
another person looking at me.
my nose scrunches up
trying really hard to look
as if this is the first time.

I want to see
what everyone else sees.
and I want to focus on
my eyes
my mouth
my nose
separately
I want to know what it is
that clues people in.
do my eyes say that I'm asian?
does my hair say that I'm native american?
does my nose say that I'm jewish?

. . .

I have decided that I
don't like to look at myself
because I don't know
what I'm seeing.

By JENNIFER CHAU, 1997
(from a longer poem
of the same title)

People seem to be more open about their prejudices around mixed-race people. This can be disturbing for the person overhearing these ugly comments—a loyalty test of sorts. Arnella, a fourteen-year-old biracial girl whose African-American friends often put down white people, best expressed this dilemma: "It's like, where do I fit in here, you know? Am I supposed to laugh? Or am I supposed to defend white people?"

THEY WOULD JUST SAY THINGS

CANDACE REA, nineteen
Kaneohe, Hawaii
Mother: European-American
Father: Filipino-American

In high school, all of my friends were cheerleaders. There were fourteen of us, and they were all Asian except for one girl who was completely white, and then me; I am mixed. I had met all of them when I was in kindergarten. When we were younger, I never thought, "They're Asian and I'm half and half." None of that mattered.

But when I got into high school, I began noticing my friends making negative comments about white people. They would say, "Those damn *haoles*," * and that white people were all stuck up, and rich, and that they all look alike.

And my Caucasian friend and I would look at each other, and then they would turn to us and say, "Oh, but you're Asian at heart." So they made a distinction between the other white people and us.

It hurt because they would just say things and wouldn't consider that I was part white. I know I look white, so when they made comments about white people, I would take it to heart, even though I knew they weren't directing them at me. And even though I'm not a full *haole,* I took it to heart because I identify with my mom so much. Sometimes I just wished that they were more sensitive.

A lot of local people hate the *haoles* even though the *haoles* have been in Hawaii for generations too. I didn't hang out with many *haole* people, so I never saw *haoles* making comments or discriminating against Filipinos. I guess there are jokes about Filipinos, but then there are jokes about every other cultural and ethnic group in Hawaii.

It was quite a shock when I came to the mainland to go to college. I know there's racial tension in Hawaii, but it doesn't seem as extreme compared to the mainland. There's so much tension between blacks and whites here. Sometimes when I walk past an African-American woman she'll look at me and I feel like she's thinking, "She's white, she's one of them." I'd just feel stereotyped into one big group.

Haole means "foreigner" in Hawaiian, but it has come to mean "white person."

There's a lot more hatred toward white people among the Asian-Americans I've met here in California. There's a club called the Asian Alliance and technically I'm a member of it because I am half Filipino. But I've never gone to any of the meetings because I know that a lot of white bashing goes on there.

People back home were like, "Okay, I'm a minority." But there were so many Asians that they weren't so strong about standing up for their rights. In Hawaii, people make comments about whites, but there's the Aloha spirit, and everyone is more accepting. People would never think to ask if I was mixed because a lot of people are mixed at home and it's not a big deal. Here, it's a big deal because there's so much clashing between the races.

HE KEPT TALKING ABOUT HOW DIRTY THEY WERE

GREG ALLEN, G.A.P. PHOTO, L.L.C.

ANGELA TONKOVICH, eighteen
White Lake, Michigan
Mother: Mexican-American
Father: European-American (Czechoslovakian)

I remember one time in my social studies class in ninth grade, we were talking about derogatory names for different races. It was a class discussion. And I sat next to this kid who went off on all the derogatory names for Mexican-Americans. He said they're "dirty spics and wetbacks." And he kept talking about how dirty they were. He just kept going on and on.

I didn't say anything. I was just shocked. Sitting next to him, I felt really strange. And I know that he didn't know that I am Mexican-American.

The teacher said, "Those are some of the terms you can use." And then we just went on. He didn't say, "You shouldn't use those terms." Later I wrote a letter to that teacher saying I didn't appreciate how he conducted his class that day. I never got an answer though.

For the rest of that class I just hated sitting next to that kid.

I ENCOUNTER THINGS LIKE THAT—CLUELESS RACISM

LISA, eighteen
Northern New Jersey
Mother: Chinese-American
Father: European-American (English)

I remember riding in a school bus once and people were making these Asian jokes. I can take a joke—sometimes levity is cute. But this girl was pushing it a little too far, definitely being insulting. And another girl turned around and said, "You know, Lisa is half Asian."

She's like, "Yeah, but she's not the real thing."

And I said, "I'm not the real thing? Half, so it doesn't count?" Even if I was completely Caucasian, it was still racist and really insulting. Somebody wouldn't dare say that in front of somebody who was completely Asian. But they'll think that by including you **161** in mocking others they're doing you a favor—like you're beyond racism, it doesn't apply to you because you're half.

If you're biracial, a lot of times people think, "Oh, you're the exception to the rule. I can make racist comments, but you won't mind because you're not really Asian. You don't really look it."

I encounter things like that—clueless racism. A lot of times, people will say, "Oh, I'm not a racist," and then they'll make these little blunders.

I think it's cool to be around them and to make them face up to what they just said, like, "I'm here, and I'm your friend, and how could you say something like that about a part of who I am—a big part of who I am?" I think just letting them know that it's insulting and that it is, in fact, racist helps them realize their mistake. And so I think you can stop a lot of that.

YOU GET TO SEE HOW NEGATIVE THE WORLD IS

AMANDA HOLZHAUER, sixteen
Cleveland Heights, Ohio
Mother: African-American
Father: European-American (German, Swiss)

Being biracial, you get the best of both worlds but you also get the worst. It makes me look at the world slightly differently. And I'm not saying that I can't be racist, but it helps to prevent that. It makes it easier for me to spot people who are being racist. If someone is being negative to whites, I pick it up. If someone is being negative toward blacks, I pick it up. If someone is being negative toward anyone, I pick it up.

But it's also kind of not fun because it makes it easier to see the world as it is. When you're hanging out with someone and they make a derogatory comment, you're like, "That's kind of ignorant." You get to see that side of people.

You get racial comments about being black, about being white, about being mixed. I get the prejudice of both sides. So you see more prejudice. And then you see the people who don't approve of interracial marriages.

You get to see how negative the world is and how ununified it is. But you still get hope from the people who aren't that way.

ROOTS: RANDOM THOUGHTS ON RANDOM HAIR

TATSU YAMATO, twenty
Seattle, Washington
Mother: African-American
Father: Japanese-American

I am twenty years old. I am in my third year of college. And you know what? I still don't know what the heck to do with my hair. Twenty years. That's a long time—that's a lot of bad hair days (a bit over 7,300).

Reenactment:

"Hello."

"Hello! Have a seat. What can I do for you today?"

"A haircut, please."

"Okay . . . um . . . (pause) . . . it says here that your name is . . . Tatsu?"

"Uh-huh."

"That's interesting. What kind of name is that?"

"Japanese."

"Oh! . . . ??? (look of consternation) . . . and that would make you . . . ?"

"Japanese and black."

". . ."

"Um . . . can I have that haircut, please?"

"Uh . . . okay" (long pause).

(click-buzzzzzzzzzzzzzzzzzzzzzzzzzz-click)

(snip snip snip . . . snip)

(click-buzzzzzzzzz-click)

(snip snip)

". . ."

(click-buzzzzzz-click)

(click-buzz-click)

(exasperated sigh)

"Is there something wrong?"

"I've never cut anything like this! Your hair is just so . . . so . . . so . . ."

Yeah . . . so like, this is my big revelation: A Supercuts place is probably not the best for a guy with my hair to invest $10.

When I was a baby, I started off with a head of straight black Japanese hair. . . . By the time I was four, my hair had developed into long bouncy light-brown curls . . . and then, somewhere along the way, it took a sharp turn toward my black heritage (i.e., nappification) but not quite enough for those cool Kid 'N Play five-foot flat-tops. . . . So now I have this wonderful head of hair that's not too nappy, not too straight, but just . . . special.

I went through many years of a rather unfortunate combination of rarely cut hair and a penchant for parting it to the side—looked kind of like Frederick Douglass's do—only *much* worse. This also happened to coincide with my emulate-Alex-on-*Family-Ties* period, where I dressed in sweater vests and clip-on bow ties for school every day. Yeah, I was a confused little boy.

Sometime in middle school, however, I began to move away from the quest to be whiter than white (symbolized for me by Alex) and cautiously toyed with the idea that "black is beautiful." So I started getting flat-tops . . . but they just didn't quite work right, either. My classmates, in that understanding and compassionate way junior high schoolers are so famous for, observed that my widow's peak granted me a striking resemblance to Eddie Munster. They nicknamed me accordingly.

One day, back when I was at Garfield High in Seattle, my friend Ethan and I hop the Metro bus at 34th and Cherry to go downtown. We proceed immediately toward our customary positions in the back corner of the bus, a place reserved for drunks, gangsters, and teenage veteran bus-riders who like to front like they's hard. However, on this day, a family of middle-school-age black folks are sitting in the back. They are loudly conversing among themselves—loud boasts, threats, and jokes flying back and forth through the air, peppering listening eardrums with assorted combinations of obscenities. Time to code-switch Hapa-boy. My walk and talk adjust slightly as I stride toward my corner seat. The cousins watch me approach and the topic of discussion becomes me—or, rather, me and my hair.

"Look at his hair!"

"Yeah, look—what's up with his head?"

"Yeah, that smack's all messed up."

I'm getting annoyed by this attention my head is receiving.

"His hair—yeah, he's mixed. See?"

The kid says, "He's mixed," as if he were exclaiming that I had soiled myself and held my dirty drawers up to his face. As I try to take my seat, one of the kids slides over and puts out his arm to bar my way. With a nasty little hateful facial expression he tells me, "You can't sit here."

"But . . . why not? Nobody's sitting here. You already got your seat."

"We don't want no half-breeds sitting here."

?!!! I quickly collect myself.

"What? I'm gonna ask you nicely. Please move."

"Wanna make me?"

"Look, man, I don't believe in this black-on-black junk but . . ."

"Try it, you zebra *$%&."

That one hits me like a crisp pimp-slap across the face. This is not going well. A little middle-school piece of garbage is successfully whipping the emotional snot out of me. I'm reeling inside and feeling light-headed. Keeping as tough and angry an expression as I can, I glare down at the kid for a bit—he's not moving, I see. So, with steely resolve, I turn around, clench my fists tightly . . . and march to the front of the bus. No black-on-black violence, but for some reason I have no problem turning brothers and sisters into the Man.

A few minutes later, I'm sitting on the bus in my corner seat, brooding over what just happened, while some angry middle-schoolers are standing at the corner of 34th and Cherry waiting for another bus. I'm angry too, but, in a sick kind of way, excited that my hair is such a visible sign of my mixed heritage.

My hair is a symbol of my identity. My hair is my pride. My hair is—an answer? I didn't even know what the questions were, but something told me that if I let my hair go long enough it would answer some questions for me that I needed to know, even though I hadn't articulated them yet.

Sometime around when I was twelve, I had a conversation with a friend of my mother's. I probably should have paid more attention at the time. My mother's friend, a Hapa black-Korean, told me that we Hapa black folk should never brush or comb our hair with anything but our fingers. And she told me that I should leave my hair wet after washing it and put in liberal amounts of hair goop.

But I didn't listen like I should have. I just looked at pictures of my hair when I was a baby and thought that if I let my hair grow out long enough it could be healthy and non-kinky, shiny, black, beautiful flowing locks. I wanted to look like some cool-ass samurai dude, his hair blowing in wisps in front of his face. Weird racial identity games were going on in my head. Secretly, I hoped that my hair would tell me which way to "swing," and even more secretly, I hoped it would swing toward the brown-black straightness of my father's Japanese head. However, as my hair grew out, it seemed pretty obvious to others that such was not going to be the case.

"Hey, man, you growing that out for dreads or something?"

"Uh, yeah. Okay."

So this was the deal with my hair: I wanted it to look like that samurai dude because I felt I already looked black enough. Shoot, my skin's kind of a dead giveaway. However, as for looking Japanese . . .

"Tatsu? What kind of name is that?"

"Japanese."

"Really? Are you part Japanese or something?"

"As a matter of fact, yes, my father is Japanese. My mother is black."

"Funny, you don't look Japanese to me; you just look black" (big dumb-ass smile).

"Ahh" (big saccharine smile) "ah, yes. Haha heh heh" (you punk).

Yeah, so see, I wanted people to just know—to feel uneasy as I walked around with my brown skin beneath a head of flowing samurai hair, messing with their conceptions of race. I wouldn't say anything. I'd just be one bold, beautiful statement of defiance against America's whack color game. Or maybe I just wanted to escape my blackness. . . .

MY SO-CALLED IDENTITY

Who am I? Where do I fit in? Those are the questions that drive teenagers and young adults to a frenzy of experimentation, reflection, and self-exploration. "They might immerse themselves in different experiences or in research as a way of trying on and finding out information," observes Maria Root. "That's all a normal part of identity development."

Since our society is so race-conscious, discovering where you fit, if you are racially mixed, can be a bit more complicated. Until recently, much of the research about mixed-race people portrayed them as tormented individuals who were torn between two worlds.

However, the experts I talked to say this is not necessarily true. Christine Iijima Hall, a social psychologist who did some of the pioneering research on mixed-race identity, notes: "The stereotypes have been that people who are racially mixed are confused and have psychological problems. But most of the people who published these studies were therapists or people who worked in psychiatric hospitals and were working with people who had problems. No one had done a study on a healthy population."

In the late 1970s, Hall studied thirty mixed-race black-Japanese people whom she recruited from the general population. The majority of them, she found, were well adjusted and had succeeded in integrating their various heritages into a healthy whole.

"If you are mixed race, I don't think that you have to identify that way," says Root. "There is no one right way to identify. Each person needs to figure that out for him- or herself. At more than any other point in history there is room to have some options about landing in a place that feels right."

On the following pages, the people I talked to share some of the tools and strategies they used to explore their identities.

YOU TRY DIFFERENT THINGS. . . . YOU REALIZE THE TRUTH

BRIAN COLWELL, twenty-three
Cupertino, California
Mother: Japanese-American
Father: European-American

When I was really young, I thought I was like everyone else. I had almost no ethnic identity. It was not defined yet, whereas now it is. So it must have developed somewhere along the way. I don't know if there was one single point where it just came together. But the fact that I was mixed was hammered into me all of my life. It was always obvious that that was what I was.

I've had experiences where I learned that I was different—that was slammed in my face. There's one experience that I remember; it was a formative experience. There was some object some kid brought to school to show his friend. It was a toy or something. The other kid couldn't find his, and because I had one just like it, they all automatically assumed that I had stolen it. It was, like, no trial, no jury—just instant conviction, finger-pointing, screaming, and yelling.

173

They called me names, like "Chinaman," and did the slanty-eyes thing. And I was totally confused, because I was completely innocent. It was like, why are they all picking on me? Later on, when I thought about it, I saw that I was being singled out specifically because of the way I look.

I still remember to this day how I felt in that situation. I felt like I was being victimized because there were all these people persecuting me for no reason. I had no idea that I was half or that I was part Asian, mixed-race, biracial, or anything. I was just myself, and suddenly, that was wrong.

I can remember times when I tried to explain my background to people and I was uncomfortable because it wasn't something I talked about that much and it was also not something I thought about. I was forced to abstract to somebody this concept that is totally normal to me. I'd go to a baseball game one day and to an Obon* festival the next. It was crazy, but it was so normal.

I guess, if I thought I was Japanese, going to Japan changed my mind. We have a sister city in Japan and they sponsored a group of twelve bright young upstanding citizens to go. It was really cool. I was twelve, fourteen, somewhere in there. I saw what real Japanese people were like and it was pretty obvious that I was not one of them.

Japanese society is real homogeneous and an outsider, a foreigner especially, stands out like a sore thumb. People stare at you. They treat you a certain way as a foreigner and they treat you another way as a Japanese person. It's just obvious if you go into a shop, from the way the shopkeeper looks at you or treats you; it's just a totally different type of demeanor.

And being there as a half-Japanese person, I was definitely on

*A Buddhist festival celebrated in Japan and by Japanese-Americans in the United States. The festival allows people to show appreciation and respect for their ancestors.

the foreigner side of the fence. Like, if I was at a temple, people would be parading around me or whispering around me. There were times when I just wanted to forget about who I was and be part of the environment and enjoy the wonderful place I was in and not have my identity be an issue.

It made me realize, "If I'm in Japan, no one is ever going to accept me as Japanese." It made me think, "Okay, check that off the list—I'm definitely not Japanese." That was maybe a little disappointing. But it wasn't such a negative thing for me, it was more of a revelatory experience.

At other times, I thought about experiences where I didn't fit in here and I thought, "Okay, I'm definitely not American either." That made me gravitate toward what I am, which is a mixture.

You lean one way and then the other. You try different things and then you find a medium where you realize the truth.

As far as racial identity goes, some of the people I spoke to were still exploring their options. I interviewed them several times over a period of one to two years, and I saw their self-definitions shift as they explored different facets of themselves. Miriam was one of these people.

OVERNIGHT, ALL THIS FILIPINO STUFF STARTED HAPPENING TO ME!

MIRIAM WARREN, sixteen
Las Vegas, Nevada
Mother: European-American (German)
Biological Father: Filipino-American
Adoptive Father: European-American

When people first meet me and then they see my mom, I can tell that they are sort of shocked, because she doesn't look like me at all. I'll say, "Oh, that's my mom—that one in the purple."

And they'll be like, "That white lady?" 'Cause they usually think that my mom's going to be Filipino.

My mom has white skin that's the color of milk and red hair, and I have brown skin and black hair. And my dad—he's white. I never met my biological father. My mom met my adoptive father, who is the person I call Dad. They had my little brother, and then they got divorced. My little brother's white. I think I look a little out of place in my family. Everyone in my family is white and I am the only one who's Asian. My little brother calls me "brown girl."

176

My mom always told me, "You are Filipino and you are German." But I never thought, "Hey, that's two different races and I'm the product of an interracial relationship." I didn't even realize that I was biracial until maybe ninth grade because I started feeling the pressure to assimilate with a certain racial group—you had blacks here, whites here, Asians over there. I liked all of the people, so I didn't want to do that. I guess that was the beginning of my quest for what my identity is and I don't think I've reached the pinnacle yet. I'm still thinking about what I am.

There are certain people who can't figure out who I am. They figure that I'm different from them because I don't just have white friends, I don't just have black friends—I have lots of different kinds of friends.

A lot of Filipino people don't automatically know, "Hey, she's Filipino." They have their own clique and I'm not a part of it. All of the Asians basically hang out together. When new Filipinos or new Asians come to the school, they take them into their groups. But they never did that with me. That's probably because I'm not like them.

I think that they are very clannish. They stick together. They are kind of quiet. They dress in a certain way. They act in a certain way. I don't dress like them, I don't act like them, and I'm a very boisterous person. I'm extremely involved in public-speaking activities. And if you see something going on at my school, most likely I'll be the leader of it. And that's just not what they are into.

I don't feel a connection to Filipinos. If I was in a crowded room and I was looking for a connection with someone, I wouldn't go up to an Asian person, because I've never been around the culture. I don't know anything about it. I don't speak the language. I identify with it and I know that that's what I am, but I don't identify with it like, "Those are my people."

177

One Year Later . . .

As I look back I realize, wow, just overnight, all this Filipino stuff started happening to me! It's basically been an explosion in the last five or six months! I had the first Asian boyfriend I ever had in my life. Now I have lots of Asian friends and a really good Asian girlfriend. We go out and we go dancing. She invites me over to her house and we hang out. Previous to that, I never had a Filipino friend. I don't even think I had an Asian friend. I had never been in an Asian house. The closest I'd ever come to Asian culture was Chinese take-out.

Well, what happened was I got turned on to the Filipino American Women's National Conference on the Internet. I was interested in writing a speech on being biracial, so they offered me a scholarship. All of a sudden, I was going to this conference and I was staying with this woman who belonged to the Filipino American Women's network chapter in Minneapolis. She has three children who are Filipino and white just like me.

I had never been surrounded by so many Filipinos in my life! I had never eaten Filipino food—all of a sudden I was eating Filipino food. I had never heard Tagalog spoken. It was like, "Wow, this is me!" But still, I was like, "I'm so different from this—this is not me. I feel so white. I'm a little brown girl growing up in a completely white family, not knowing what this whole Filipino thing is."

So then I went home and I was still mulling it over. In January, I went to this dance at my friend's high school. I would always see this Asian clique, as I call it, and I would think, "Wow, I'm just totally not like that. I could never go talk to them." But I saw Jenny from my first-grade class and I was like, "Maybe I'll just say hi." She introduced me to all of these Filipino people. Then all of

a sudden, I was asked to the prom by a Filipino guy. And I became friends with his friends. Pretty soon we were all going to lunch together.

Then one night I was at a restaurant and I saw this really cute Filipino guy and gave him my number. We dated for a while and I would go over to his house a lot. Of course, his parents were Filipino. They would cook Filipino food. Almost all of his friends are Filipino. It didn't work out between us, but that was another gateway for me to see what being Filipino is like. It gave me sort of an "in" to the culture because I had a lot of book knowledge about being Filipino but I really needed to feel it, to be near Filipinos, to be in their homes.

So now I have a wide group of Asian friends who I hang out with all the time. Now I'm pretty much a part of the clique.

I think that, before, they just didn't understand who I was and they weren't opening themselves up to me. So I decided, "Hey, I need to get in there, I need to speak their language, see what makes them tick. And once I learn more about them, I can easily become friends with them." So that's exactly what I did and that's exactly what happened.

It's still really new to me. But now, most of the time, I feel, "I'm a part of this. I'm Filipino." It's becoming more a part of me every single day. And I'm just really proud of my culture and I'm so happy that I'm Filipino. I wish my parents had tried to expose me to it in the past. But learning it on my own isn't too bad either.

Other people—white friends, Hispanic friends, black friends— say, "What's up with this whole Asian thing? How come all of a sudden you have a lot of Asian friends? Are you trying to be Asian?"

And I would say, "You know, I've been Asian ever since I was born." I think that people who say things like that just don't understand, and I've tried to explain to them: "I've been doing a lot **179** of research and I've found out a lot about being Filipino and I am really happy about it."

I say, "You don't understand because you're not both." I don't think people are going to go up to either of my best friends and say, "Um, what nationality are you?" or "What race are you?" or "What's your ethnicity?" But people are going to ask me that every single day, sometimes more than once a day. If someone is white, or if they are black, or if they are Hispanic, or if they are full Filipino, they wake up every morning and they know that. They may question themselves about life. They may question themselves about what path they are on. But they never question themselves as to "What am I?" They know, and in most cases, their parents are the same thing.

Last week, I met my biological father for the first time. He has a really, really thick accent and, of course, he is brown, kind of like me. My best friend came to dinner with us and she said, "You have the same nose as him."

I love pictures. I carry this huge photo album around in my backpack. But what I've always wanted is to have a photo album, like all of my friends do, that I can look at and say, "I have my dad's smile." Or "I have this from my mom." And not having that has been a hard thing. I don't look anything like my mom. But I guess I look a little bit like my dad. Now I'll be able to have that.

"WHY DON'T YOU GO OUT WITH ANY WHITE GIRLS?"

KURTIS FUJITA, twenty
Agoura Hills, California
Mother: European-American (Irish, English)
Father: Japanese-American (Hawaiian)
Stepfather: European-American

I was born in Hawaii and lived there until I was seven. My parents got divorced. Then my mother took me and my sister to L.A., to a place called Agoura Hills. It's kind of a preppy place, predominantly a Caucasian-Jewish community, very suburban upper-middle class.

I didn't realize how clueless people were about different cultures until I moved to Agoura. I said I was from Hawaii and they thought I had lived in a little grass hut and hunted pigs. People in Agoura grouped all Asians into one big mess. They thought Korean people spoke Chinese. They made insulting, ignorant comments. I was called a "gook" once; I was called a "Chink." People would imitate what they thought was an Asian accent.

It was funny, because in high school I really got into Chinese culture. I'd go to Los Angeles and spend the whole day in Chinatown. One of my friends was Thai and he showed me Hong Kong movies. Chinese guys were the main actors. I thought, "The Asian guy's the romantic interest, the action hero. What a novel idea!" It was the first time I saw Asians depicted in film, and not as idiots. Asians were not book-reading geeks with the pocket protectors and calculators. I thought that was so cool. So every day after **181** school I'd drive a good forty minutes into the city to find a store. I'd rent Chinese movies. And then I'd drive back.

Now I'm in San Francisco and it's a whole different environment. It's almost like going back to Hawaii because there is such a predominant Asian community here. Almost all of the girls I've gone out with since I've been here have been Asian. My ex-girlfriend asked me why. And all of a sudden I was thinking about what my mom had said, "What's wrong with American girls? Why aren't you going out with any American girls?" Even my sister says, "Why don't you go out with any white girls?" I can't explain it and I don't know why it's such an issue. It's awkward for me.

My mother is real open-minded but every now and then she says things and I feel guilty. Like she called me and asked me what I was doing for the Fourth of July. I said I was going to hang out with my friend Fred, and we were going to do kung fu. And she said, "Try and do something American today for a change—get a hot dog and Coca-Cola." I was surprised that she said that. I don't feel that American necessarily means hot dogs and Coca-Cola and hamburgers and baseball and all that. People think that American means white Anglo-Saxon. There is no question in my mind that being Asian means being American.

As much as I hate to admit it, I get very confused. Because I'm very close to my mom and my stepdad, sometimes I'll feel guilty that I'm interested in Asian culture a lot more than Caucasian culture. I always feel like I'm betraying the Caucasian side of my heritage. Sometimes there are questions in my mind about which side I relate to more or which side I should relate to more. I think a lot of that comes from my parents' divorce, because after that there was a split, too, from Hawaii and that side of the family and that part of my cultural identity.

182

Ten Months Later . . .

I spent a lot of time in Chinatown, because it was so different and I really enjoy the culture. But after hanging out there for a while, I realized that that wasn't completely me either.

I guess to some degree I have been trying to force myself to fit into one or the other. Now the way I feel is—I am both. If I like something, I don't question, "Is that being too Asian?" or "Is that being too Caucasian?" I don't feel the need to distinguish between them anymore. I don't feel I have to worry about it anymore. In a way, I'm lucky because I can fit into so many places.

Each person has to find their own identity. You can find your own identity through tons of different ways. I think there are things that transcend racial barriers and racial boundaries. To me, there is something spiritual about doing kung fu or drawing; there is something that I feel. And I define myself by those actions—by what I do and what I feel—not by any standard of ethnicity.

I don't think anybody should limit themselves as to what they are. I don't think anybody can ever say, "I am this." You're always changing, there's a new definition for you every second. You've got to keep learning, or else you might as well be dead 'cause you're not doing anything with your life.

Anton Hart, a clinical psychologist and psychoanalyst in New York City, who is Jewish and African-American, believes that "you don't have to feel obligated to keep all parts of your heritage equal at all times." If you are racially mixed, grabbing hold of and affirming one part of your heritage for a period of time can be a natural and necessary part of coming to terms with your identity. In order to get the most out of a new experience, "you may have to put other things aside temporarily." **183**

When mixed-race people experiment with culture and race, other people, particularly parents, may become alarmed. Kurtis's mom suggested that he do something "American." Miriam's friends asked, "What's up with this whole Asian thing?" People may think, "Why is this kid simply emphasizing one side? Why is this kid throwing aside half of who he or she is?" They may worry, "Will I be rejected?"

"Parents would be making a mistake if they said, 'My kid is going too far in this direction, I have to bring him back and balance it out,' " says Hart. "It will find its balance."

Maria Root agrees. "Shifting back and forth between ethnic or racial groups is a natural thing to do as a way of trying to find out where you fit, who you are, and what works." Trying on different styles and images is something that all young people do—not just racially mixed people. "It's just more heavily scrutinized and more obvious when we do it around race and culture or ethnicity.

"It's a way to experiment. You keep changing hats and eventually you might make your own hat. I encourage people to experiment."

The sociologist Teresa Kay Williams also sees adolescence as "a crucial time for people to try on different identities." But she adds that young people need to feel good about all parts of their heritage. For example, Williams, who has interviewed many mixed-race people in her research, has found that some of them reject or minimize their European ancestry in response to experiencing white racism:

"People who are part white start taking on guilt in the same way that white Americans probably do. Like, 'I've got to beat myself up because I'm the bad white person,' or 'I have to be this super person of color.'

184

"A healthy multiracial identity for people who are part white means being able to feel comfortable about that whiteness as well, and to appreciate it and to love it and to claim it and not have to apologize to anybody for it."

MY CENTRAL CORE IDENTITY ISN'T IMMERSED IN RACE

MAYA COREY, nineteen
Minneapolis, Minnesota
Mother: European-American (German)
Father: African

When my mom was looking for a home, she wanted a place where I would feel comfortable. That's why she chose to stay in the city even though she prefers the country. And where we ended up—half of the people are biracial or are in biracial families. In the Twin Cities area, it's the norm almost. I go home now and every other couple I see is interracial and I see these little mixed kids.

I knew I was a little bit different. And I thought, "I'm lucky to be both—black and white." Other kids knew that there was white, there was black, and there was mixed. At different times, I can remember wanting to be blond or kind of white. But I think a lot of black kids have that experience. I grew out of it eventually.

In seventh grade I went to the International School of Minnesota. There was a mixture of white students, minority students, **185** and international students. You didn't have the white-black issue because it was so international and that was good.

There was a program at school for black issues. I was put into that category even though everyone knew my mother. And it was weird because we would discuss our experiences with society and I felt, "Do I really have a valid black experience? I was raised by a white mother, and I wasn't raised with my father, so what is my culture?"

When I came to Duke, I ended up with a black roommate and we found other black people. So that's who I ended up hanging out with, who my friends are. I haven't really gotten to know any white people, even in my hall.

It's definitely been a strange experience—I had gone to a school where some of my best friends were white and Asian and whatnot, then I came to this school and I only hang out with black people. That is where I feel most comfortable, but it's weird. I don't think of myself as fitting in with black people only.

At Duke the majority of people are white and I want to somehow have a connection with them. But they don't really want to get to know us. At Duke, for the first time in my life, people don't know that I am biracial. So when my mom came to my school at the end of the year, other girls in my hall were kind of surprised. I was glad that they knew. I felt that acknowledging that I'm biracial would explain that I know both sides. I thought maybe the white people would accept me more. I want people to know that I am biracial sometimes.

I don't know what I want my image to be yet. Around eighth grade, I wanted people to see me as black for a while. And then suddenly now, I want to be biracial. I look at different models in the spotlight, like Halle Berry. She says she is black even though

her mother is white because our society is going to view her as a black person. Then there's Mariah Carey, who acknowledges all aspects of her identity. Sometimes I have to make a decision, whether it's filling out a form or how I explain myself, and I think about these issues.

And I definitely want to be accepted as black by the black community. I don't want my friends to think I'm trying to be better than them or different. But at the same time, I'd like to acknowledge my heritage and who my mother is. I have another experience that's a little bit different because I was raised by a white person. So that's a very important part of who I am and I can't ignore that and deny that fact.

There are negative experiences for all people. As a biracial person, it's struggling to make people believe that I fit in, or even knowing where I want to fit in. I definitely went through that stage that I think a lot of biracial people go through. Black people don't completely accept me because I'm lighter, or because my mom is white. And white people don't accept me because I'm not white. So where do I fit in? That definitely was hard.

I've had people say, "You were not raised by a black family, and you are educated, and your mom makes good money, so why do you get to go to that minority program?" One of my friends said that to me. Or on affirmative action they say, "Why should that apply to you?" Just people saying, "You don't belong"—that's the type of thing that's been negative.

It's not fair for people to say that because you're biracial you're not black. They can't say that we're not black because of the experience that we're going to have. There are so many different kinds of black people—you can be from the Islands, you can be from Africa, you can be African-American. I think I'm part of the whole so-called American black world experience. So that's the point that I've come to. **187**

One and a Half Years Later . . .

I think I wasn't sure who I was before. I was a little confused because I couldn't separate who I was from how other people viewed me. I think that's something all adolescents and young people go through on some level. I guess it's part of growing up.

For a while I think I was consumed with the racial aspect of my identity. When I thought about what made me who I was, I used to think that it largely had to do with race. Although I still see that as an important factor, I don't see it as a confusing factor anymore. I have found so many other things at this stage in my life that have helped me direct my identity, like: What will my career be? What type of person do I want to be? What's my spiritual base? What can I offer to the world or to my community? I think race has become, not less important, but less the main focal point.

I better understand the politics of race and how it plays out here in America. So I've become more comfortable acknowledging my blackness and more comfortable with the fact that people aren't going to know who my mother is and they're just going to know who I am most of the time. So my experiences are going to be more similar to a black person's.

I do consider myself black and I am very comfortable doing so. That's not saying that in considering myself black I am denying my biracial heritage. Similar to Halle Berry, I realize that, when I step outside of my homeplace, people are going to see me as black. They're going to treat me, good or bad, as a black person, and I have to consider what that means both historically and socially.

I realize that race, to me, is more something that I react to and deal with on the outside than something that I create for myself. It's a part of the external identity that we all have—that social identity or even political identity. It has nothing to do with my internal identity. I think what's clearer for me today is that my internal identity has to do with all of those other things I talked about—my goals, my spiritual ideology, et cetera. Being biracial or being black really doesn't have a lot to do with those things.

I took a class last semester where we talked about identity and race a lot. Something we talked about is that there is a core essence to people that is kind of unchangeable. How you view yourself, how you treat yourself, what your goals are, what you want to do in the world, what you feel your place is, what moves you, what drives you, are simply separate from all societal things—race, class, and other labels. My central core identity isn't immersed in race.

I'm realizing that my role in the Duke community has had to do with multiculturalism, bringing people together. I sit on the President's Council on Black Affairs and a residence-life planning group that's reshaping the entire vision for residence life at Duke. A lot of that is based on problems of race relations and diversity and inclusivity. And so I've been sitting with some great minds and working out issues of race and people coming together, and I think it's indirectly given me a lot of insight about those things.

I've got a long way to go, but I've come to a point where I'm very comfortable with how I consider myself. To be honest, it came from self-confidence and realizing that all those things—societal definitions and limits regarding racial identity and other labels—don't have to have anything to do with the inside of me. I think I just grew up.

I'M DOING A LOT OF GRAPPLING WITH CONFLICTING FEELINGS

MEILINA WILKINSON, twenty-one
Farmingdale, New York
Mother: Taiwanese
Father: European-American (English)

My parents were divorced when I was three. My father had custody of me, and my mother and her family became estranged from me.

I grew up on Long Island. It was a pretty white suburban type of experience. When I was younger, I was very Caucasian-looking. I had green eyes and blond hair and I was always considered to be an exotic-looking white girl.

I identified as more white than Asian because that was my experience then—that was who my friends were, that was what they considered me. They didn't really acknowledge that I was part Asian. So people felt comfortable making racial jokes and offensive remarks in front of me because it was not so obvious that I was part Asian.

I would hear really offensive things about how Asians look strange and how Asians talk funny and that they're kind of nerdy. So I internalized this shame about it, about being mixed. I basically didn't like myself; I wished that I were white. It got to the point where I was ashamed to tell people. I was just growing up **190** trying to be part of the in crowd.

When I went to college I started to think about race. I met people and they would ask me what my ethnicity was. I would tell them and they would say, "Are you in touch with your roots?" That always bothered me.

I think I have a lot more learning to do about this issue or just a lot more thinking to do. I'm just now trying to learn about Asian culture. I joined an Asian-American club at my college. I've been trying to read anything I can get my hands on. I'm interested in Eastern medicine, movies from Hong Kong, and acupuncture. I'm going to Beijing to study the language. It's your choice whether or not to identify with one particular group, but I think it's important to acknowledge all of yourself.

I'm doing a lot of grappling with conflicting feelings. It's hard to be very clear about it right now. There are so many gray areas—it's not just black and white.

One Year Later . . .
I'm glad I went to China. I had a really good time. I studied Mandarin. I learned enough Mandarin to say I can speak okay. I met my mother's family for the first time in seventeen years too. I went to see them in Taiwan. It is a huge, enormous family—aunts and uncles, my grandparents, and tons of cousins. They stared at me a lot because they were so shocked to see me. They said I look a lot like my mother, that I hold my chopsticks the same way, and walk the same way. I found out that she had owned a restaurant in Taiwan and that she was very independent and creative. I was really proud to hear that. My mother passed away seven years ago and so it was also very sad.

It was very intense to go from being in this comfortable routine and then suddenly it's shaken up. It was emotionally draining. When I returned to school the next semester, I was distracted and **191** a little bit depressed because I had so much to think about. I formed these bonds that I didn't expect to.

But I think now I have a bit more clarity about my family and personal issues with them, as well as about being biracial. I'm not wondering so much anymore.

In exploring their identity, it's common for people to go back to their roots—to research family history and to track down extended family members the way Meilina did, observes George Kitahara Kich, a psychologist in Berkeley, California, who has studied and written about identity formation in racially mixed people.

Among the young people I talked to, pilgrimages to far-flung places to meet long-lost relatives, or to experience a part of their cultural heritage firsthand, were common. Stefanie Liang, who has a Chinese parent, also studied Mandarin in Beijing. Denise Hobson lived in Ireland one semester; her father is Irish and her mother is Native American. Eric Stowe, Tatsu Yamato, Mitzi Carter, and Rocky Mitarai, each of whom have a Japanese parent, are currently teaching English in Japan. Travel is a revelation for people in search of themselves.

IT'S GOOD TO SEE OTHER PEOPLE WHO ARE LIKE YOU

SARA B. BUSDIECKER, twenty-six
East Lansing, Michigan
Mother: European-American (German)
Father: European-American (German)
Sara is racially mixed and adopted.

The way that I've identified has certainly changed over my lifetime. I haven't labeled myself in the same way. I don't think I've been perceived by others in the same way. It's always changing, always evolving.

When I was an infant, my parents went to a parents' group for white parents who had adopted black or multiracial children. The leaders of the group told the parents, "Your children are black; don't call them mixed." It was the seventies. You had to have solidarity, and say "Black is beautiful." So growing up, they told me that I was black or African-American. I remember feeling uncomfortable with that as a child and thinking, "How come I'm so much lighter than other black people?" and "How come people always ask me what I am?"

Now that I'm in college, in graduate school, I've come into contact with more mixed people. I think that has helped me assert my own mixed-race identity, which feels like the right fit, the most accurate way for me to identify. Since I didn't know any **193** mixed people when I was in high school or when I was a little kid, it didn't occur to me to identify that way.

"Comfortably mixed" is where I'm at now. I've finally found the word that encompasses my entire life experience—*mixed*. Now when people ask me what I am, I can give that word. And even though they don't know what it means, I know what it means.

The Mixed Initiative student group has definitely made an impact on me because I see that other people have had the same experiences. So I think that's been a big influence in my wanting to identify as mixed as opposed to anything else.

Not everyone in the group identifies as mixed. A lot of the people who are black and white, for instance, say they're black. And that's fine—not everyone has to identify as mixed or call themselves mixed. It's great just to see that there are other people who have parents and families that are of different races. It can only help you clarify your own identity.

So many people who are white, black, Asian, or what have you, take for granted that they're going to see people like themselves on the streets, and on television, and in books and newspapers. Whereas if you're mixed, that never happens. You could be in the presence of somebody who is mixed and you'd never know it. So you can feel very isolated.

Since I organized this year's mixed conference, I've had people say to me, "So you're really into this mixed thing, aren't you?" I found that to be an annoying comment. And I wondered if the same thing was said to black students who go to black student union meetings or Asian students who organize an Asian cultural event. Do people say, "So you're really into this Asian thing, aren't you?" I really doubt that that happens to other minorities.

But because this mixed identity isn't legitimate yet and people

don't recognize it, they can't understand why you would organize an event and have a group. And if you do, somehow that's wrong and you're trying too hard to identify with this mixed thing, which doesn't really exist.

The most valuable thing people can do is to try to find other people who are mixed. Start a group in your high school or in your neighborhood. The Mixed Initiative here—we're not a support group, we don't sit around talking about being mixed all the time. It just comes up casually. It's a social group. It's good to see other people who are like you, it's invaluable.

WE OPEN EACH OTHER'S EYES

STUART HAY, twenty
Fond du Lac, Wisconsin
Mother: Guyanese (West Indian)
Father: Canadian (Scottish, Irish, French)

A lot of the students here [University of Wisconsin, Madison] are from small towns in northern Wisconsin that are 100 percent white. They come to our school and see students of color and think, "Holy cow, I just saw a Chinese person and a black person today in my class. This place has got so much culture, it's unbelievable!" They are not aware of what it's like to be a person of color. They see people who support affirmative action as raising trouble—being whiners or something.

If you don't get involved in student organizations, you can feel very isolated here. So I went to a BSU [Black Student Union] meeting with a friend of mine. He's a black guy from Chicago. When we walked in there together, a bunch of black guys came up and acknowledged him. They said hi and introduced them- **195** selves and everything. They didn't even make eye contact with me. I kind of felt like an invisible person; I wasn't even there.

The reason we formed the mixed student group is because we got fed up with the BSU meetings. A lot of people have problems with them. They're very exclusive. The girls will say, "We don't like seeing our guys getting snagged up by all of those white women."

Can you imagine what it's like for mixed people to hear that? That's like us—our families are who they despise. So we can't relate to them on those issues. We like the people in the BSU, we get along. But in some ways we're very different.

It's fun relating to other people on campus who are mixed. We open each other's eyes. There are a lot of people who share the same experiences. It strengthens our awareness of being mixed as something real.

I FELT A LOT STRONGER IN WHO I WAS

MITZI UEHARA CARTER, twenty-three
Houston, Texas
Mother: Japanese-American (Okinawan)
Father: African-American

I've always been interested in different cultures. It started in second grade when I saw a TV show and they advertised for pen pals. I had a lot of pen pals from all over—Canada, Kuwait. They opened my eyes to the world around me and increased my curiosity.

My senior year, I got my mom to host an exchange student from Brazil. She was my age and she went to my school. I learned a lot from her. Her perception of me as "mulatta" or "morena" was interesting. She would say, "Why would you call yourself black (which I did on occasion) when you're so much better?" I learned then that black had a stigma, a negative connotation, in Brazil, yet "mixing" was celebrated.

It seemed somewhat ironic. I became more curious about how people were treated around the world, what perceptions about racial mixing had developed internationally, what similarities blacks across the globe had, and how globalization has affected these things.

197

I went into college as a premed. I wanted to be a doctor, or a veterinarian, something in the sciences. Then I took my first cultural anthropology class and I was like, "Wow, this is it!" I knew it was what I wanted to focus on. I took more classes, especially classes focusing on race and identity. We looked at Afro-Brazilian culture. We looked at Okinawa—it was interesting to see the influence of American military bases on Okinawan culture and how it's changed over the last fifty years. Cultural anthropology is about documenting that.

I wrote several papers on being biracial. I did papers on the Punjabi-Mexicans in California. People from the Punjab in India migrated to California to pick oranges. I was amazed when we learned how the Mexican women and Punjabi men mixed and how their children identified themselves. I was like, "Whoa, it's not just me." Because cultural anthropology is about exploring identity and how identities shift, it was a great tool for helping me learn about the world and explore my own identity.

Seeing what other people go through and how all these different experiences shape their identities made me reflect on the experiences I've had that shaped my identity. And I felt a lot stronger in who I was. I felt more comfortable with who I was than I ever had been. When people asked me, "Why don't you choose?" I became stronger in my answer—"I'm not one, I'm both."

Like Mitzi, many of the college students I spoke to were majoring in subjects such as anthropology, sociology, political science, psychology, and ethnic studies. It's not a coincidence that mixed-race people are drawn to these fields and often excel in them. The subject matter of social sciences includes race, ethnicity, culture, and identity—concepts that racially mixed young people have had to deal with their entire lives. So studying and doing research in the social sciences is a way for them to make sense of their experiences and explore their identities.

I THOUGHT I HAD SETTLED THE WHOLE THING

MONINA DIAZ, twenty
Monrovia, California
Mother: African-American
Father: Puerto Rican

When I came to the end of my high school years, I remember being content in who I was because I had completely explored being black, completely explored being Hispanic. I didn't care anymore that the black girls said that I wanted to be white or that I was different. I was like, "I am black and Puerto Rican, Puerto Rican and black—and if you can't accept that, that's just too bad." I thought I had settled the whole thing.

The strange thing is that a lot of the issues that I had as a teenager have come up again. Since this semester began, and I've done all of this research,* I've had that pressure to align myself one way or the other again, as far as being either black or Puerto Rican. I remember saying, "If I was just black, it would be so much easier," or "If I was just Puerto Rican, it would be so wonderful." I thought I had put away wanting to be just black or wanting to be just Puerto Rican. I remember talking to this guy;

---

*In the chapter Check One Box, Monina talked about researching a multiracial category for the 2000 census as a school project.

he's black and white. I told him that by the end of the year I was going to settle this whole thing and I was going to choose. He laughed.

All of those issues have been raised again when I thought I'd forgotten about them. I think it came from talking to people and realizing that just because I've come to the realization that I'm both Puerto Rican and black doesn't mean that everyone else has. It came from all the reading I did on what other mixed people thought, how they felt. Before that, I didn't think anyone understood what I was saying or thinking, or that anyone else even had these thoughts. After I read all of these things, I said, "Wow, they think the same things I do or feel the same things I do."

So what brought it all up was that I had sympathizers, through what I read, who understood what I was saying and validated what I was feeling. And then I saw the need to press the importance of this on to those in my class who were like, "If you're black, you're black. One drop." That's how it was brought to the forefront again. I had to deal with that again.

The thing that was interesting for me was that these issues continue even though you think you've settled them and you've put them away. They can flare up again when you're reminded of having to choose, or of not fitting into a group. They aren't really ever settled. You're going to continue to deal with them for a long time until our society changes.

I think people can definitely just refuse to deal with any of this. I know people who have done that—just refused to deal with ethnic issues altogether, although they're obviously there. But when somebody asks you, "What are you?" it's going to be in your face. You can refuse to tangle with it. But I think that's kind of hard.

It's not unusual for identity issues to resurface years after they have supposedly been ironed out, notes psychologist George Kich. Events throughout life can trigger the question "Who am I?" Marriage is one of these, as is choosing a place to live, or having a child. The good news is that these issues often get easier to work out as you get older.

One of the strategies Monina used to define her racial identity was to name it. She uses the word Blatina *or* Latinegra *to describe herself. Because there are few positive terms in our vocabulary to describe people of mixed racial background, they have come up with their own. In the following essay, Mitzi Carter, who describes herself as* Blackanese, *explains why this word sums up her experience and why it is empowering.*

ON BEING BLACKANESE

By MITZI UEHARA CARTER, twenty-three
Houston, Texas
Mother: Japanese-American (Okinawan)
Father: African-American

"Umm . . . excuse me. Where are you from?"

"I'm from Houston, Texas."

"Oh . . . but your parents, where are they from?"

(Hmm. Should I continue to play stupid or just tell them?)

"My dad is from Houston, and my mom is from Okinawa, Japan."

"And your dad is black, then?"

"Yup."

"So do you speak Japanese?"

"Some."

"Wow. Say something."

I cannot count the number of times I've pulled this script out to rehearse with random people who have accosted me in the past. "That's so exotic, so cool that you're mixed."

It's not that these questions or comments bother me or that I am offended by their bluntness. It's more the bewilderment and the perceived exoticism of my being and the slight bossiness to do something "exotic" that annoy me. I think I am also annoyed because I am still exploring what it means to be both Japanese and black and still have difficulty trying to express what that means to others.

In many ways and for many years I have grappled with the idea of being a product of two cultures brought together by an unwanted colonization of my mother's homeland of Okinawa by American military bases. It's the invisible bug that itches under my skin every now and then. It itches when I read about Okinawan girls being raped by U.S. servicemen, when I see mail-order bride ads, when I see the half-hidden looks of disgust directed at my mother by other Japanese women when I walk by her side as a daughter.

Our bodies, our presence, our reality are a nuisance to some because we defy a definite and demarcated set of boundaries. We confuse those who try to organize ethnic groups by highlighting these boundaries because they don't know how to include us or exclude us. We are Blackanese, Hapa, Eurasian, multiracial.

My mother has been the target of jokes and derogatory comments since my older sister was born. She was the one who took

my sister by the hand and led her through the streets of Bangkok and Okinawa as eyes stared and people gathered to talk about the sambo baby. She was the one who took my siblings and me to the grocery store, the mall, the park, school, Burger King, the hospital, and church. In each of these public arenas, we were stared at—either in fascination because we were a new "sight," or with looks of disgust, or both.

Nigga-chink, black-Jap, black-Japanese mutt. The neighborhood kids, friends, and adults labeled my siblings and me with these terms especially after they recognized that my mother was completely intent on making us learn about Okinawan culture. On New Year's Day, we had black-eyed peas and mochi. We cleaned the house to start the year fresh and clean. "Don't laugh with your mouth too wide and show your teeth too much," my mom would always tell us. "Be like a woman." I had not realized that I covered my mouth each time I laughed until someone pointed it out to me in my freshman year in college.

When we disobeyed my mother's rules or screamed, we were being too "American." If I ever left the house with rollers in my hair, my mom would say I shouldn't do American things. "*Agijibiyo* [oh, Lord] . . . where you learn this from? You are Okinawan too. *Damedesuyo* [don't do that]. Don't talk so much like Americans; listen first." My mother always told us: never be too direct, never accept gifts from people on the first offer, and always be humble and modest. Those were several other cultural traits and values that I had inevitably inherited (and cherish) being raised by a Japanese mother.

Growing up in an all-black neighborhood and attending predominantly black and Latino schools until college influenced my identity also. I was definitely not accepted in Japanese circles as Japanese, for several reasons. But this is not to say that the black community I associated with embraced me as Blackanese, even **203** though I think it is more accepting of multiracial people than probably any other group (because of the one-drop rule, et cetera). Those who wish to accept all the parts of their heritage with equal weight are still excluded. And there is also a subtle push to identify more with one's black heritage than with the other part because "society won't see you as mixed or Japanese but *black*." I can't count the number of times I have heard this argument.

What I do know is that no one can tell me that I am more of one culture than another because of the way someone else defines me. I am Blackanese—a mixture of the two in ways that cannot be divided. My body and mentality are not split down the middle where half is black and the other half is Japanese. I have taken aspects of both worlds to create my own worldview and identity.

My father, on the other hand, never sat down to "teach" us about being black. We were surrounded by blackness and lived it. He was always tired when he came home from work. He'd sit back in his sofa and blast his jazz. My mom would be in the kitchen with her little tape player listening to the Japanese and Okinawan tapes my aunt sent every other month from California.

My siblings and I would stay at my grandmother's house once in a while (she cooked the best collard greens), and when my mom came to pick us up she'd teach her how to cook a Southern meal for my father. Our meals were an indicator of how much my mom held on to her traditions. My father made his requests for chicken, steak, or okra and my mom learned to cook these things. But we always had Japanese rice on the side with nori [dried seaweed] and tofu and fishcake with these really noisome beans that are supposed to be good for you (according to my mom, who knows what every Japanese magazine has to say about food and health).

It was my mother who told us that we would be discriminated against because of our color, and it was my Japanese mother to whom we ran when we were called niggers at the public swimming pool in Houston. To say to this woman, "Mom, we are just black," would be a disrespectful slap in the face. The woman who raised us and cried for years from her family's coldness and rejection because of her decision to marry interracially cried when my father's sister wouldn't let her be a part of the family picture because she was a "Jap"; this woman, who happens to be my mother, will never hear "Mom, I'm just black" from my mouth, because I'm not, and no person, society, or government will force me to say that and deny my reality and my being, no matter how offensive I am to their country or how much of a nuisance I am to their cause. I am Blackanese.

This essay was used with permission from Mitzi Carter and the Interracial Voice *online magazine.*

"OH, HE'S SOMETHING ELSE"

DEANA RABIAH

SALADIN ALI AHMED, twenty-two
Dearborn, Michigan
Mother: European-American (Irish)
Stepmother: European-American
Father: Arab-American

I grew up in Detroit and in Dearborn, which is adjacent to Detroit and has the largest Arab population outside of the Middle
East. I grew up in the south end of Dearborn, which is about 90
percent Arab.

We were two blocks from Henry Ford's main plant, the River
Rouge plant, his first big factory. That was the dominating presence in the neighborhood. It is a really interesting place because
there are all of these Arabic stores and a big mosque with a big
green dome juxtaposed against this big ugly industrial zone.
Most of the people in the neighborhood were immigrants, pretty
poor, and worked at the car factory.

We moved from that part of Dearborn to the east end of Dearborn. The east end is still majority Arab, probably about 60 to 70
percent. But it was mainly Lebanese and mainly merchant-class
people as opposed to laborers.

My father was born in Brooklyn. His mother was born in
Lebanon. His father was born in Egypt and came over here to

sell Arabic-language records. My mother was Irish. She passed away when I was about seven, and my father met another woman. She had three kids of her own from her previous marriage. She was also white and her kids were white and they became my stepbrothers and stepsister. And then my father and my stepmother had a child together. Our family is a really interesting combination.

I'm fairly light-skinned. If I'm in Detroit, the racial dynamics tend to get broken down into this weird black-white binary. So white people and black people assume that I'm white until they hear my name and then I'm something weird that's not black or white in their eyes. But then in Ann Arbor, where people are used to people with a lot of different backgrounds, people tend to be more conscious of the fact that I'm probably something other than European.

People don't confront me because of the way I look. Sometimes I'll be wearing an Arabic scarf, or something that marks me, and then people get nervous. If somebody sees my name written down, they realize, "Oh, he's something else, Arabic or Muslim or whatever." And then I have to deal with all of the baggage and the ignorance that people have. People start asking questions about terrorism or the way women are treated in Islam based on the stereotypes that are prevalent about Arabs.

That's happened a lot, especially in Detroit where there's a really visible Arab community. People would make comments: "These people smell bad" or "They're rude" or "They have too many kids" or whatever.

I used to just say, "Well, I'm Arab," and then let it go. But now, whenever I hear people say something like that, I won't let them get away with much. I'll kind of start hollering.

My father is fairly dark. Around his neighborhood, people

know he's Arab. He and I got chased out of a bar in Kentucky one time. We just went up to the counter to get a drink and the bartender said, "Look, we don't want any trouble, but we really don't like Mexes in here." And it was like this bar full of good old boys, so we decided to make a strategic exit. We weren't gonna tell them, "No, we're actually camel jockeys." Because I'm light-skinned, I don't deal with that kind of raw confrontation very often, so it made me angry. After a while it was just humorous. I think my dad's more used to that kind of stuff than I am.

My dad and I talk about it quite a bit actually. He used to work at the Ford factory, and while he was working there, he, along with some other people in the community, started up this community center for Arab immigrants. He was involved in a lot of social movements. He knew a lot of people who were Black Panthers or American Indian Movement people. My dad's friends were of all races. And so he's very conscious of racist stuff and I was raised with a lot of those liberal and/or radical ideas about race.

I started to think more about race in high school. I read Malcolm X and a lot of different stuff that had to do with race and racism and I think I started trying to figure it out. There were different things that happened during high school—the Gulf War, the L.A. riots, and some other things—where race was prevalent in the way they were discussed in the media. So I think I started trying to figure out where I fit in with these concepts that were being discussed on TV.

A lot of ugly racism came out around the Gulf War. I remember some little poster that some kid stuck up around school. It had a gun sight and in the gun sight was a drawing of a stereotypical Arab on a camel and it said, "I'd fly 10,000 miles to smoke a camel." There were a lot of nasty jokes like that. In the media, Saddam Hussein was portrayed as a fanatic, or a terrorist, and that was linked to the fact that he is an Arab.

Seeing that stuff started to make me think more consciously about the fact that I am an Arab. And yet I had this other side to me—it was undeniable that I was white also, and a lot of my friends were white.

Once I got out of high school, I started to think about this more and more. I realized how distanced I was in a lot of ways from my Arabness and I worked really hard to go in the opposite direction, to an almost silly degree, where I was only hanging out with Arabs or other people of color. I wouldn't hang out with white people that much. And I made conscious choices about the music I listened to—Arab or black music. I had listened to more white music, or mainstream rock and roll, when I was in high school. And the way I dressed changed a little bit. My clothes were associated with hip-hop. The clothes I wore in high school were associated with alternative music. I think I was consciously trying to not be white. And that lasted a little while.

Actually that's when I started writing poetry a lot; I wrote to try to resolve things. I can't stress enough how important that was as far as sorting out some of the different things that were going on in my head.

My biracial identity is something I'm probably going to be negotiating my whole life. But it's not anything that bothers me anymore. Most of my friends are Arab, or black, or Asian, but that hasn't been a conscious choice. It's just that that's the social scene that I've been into. A lot of my friends are white also. There's no longer a consciousness of whiteness that used to be there.

My major is American culture. It's an interdisciplinary program. It's got aspects of sociology, ethnic studies, American history, literature—all of these things rolled into one. I've been interested in doing research on Arab-American communities. There's really not much acknowledgment of Arab-Americans even though there are, by some reports, three million of us in this country.

Arabs are in a very strange position in that, in some areas, we are regarded as white to a certain extent. And then in other areas, like in the South during Jim Crow, several Arab-Americans were lynched because they were "looking" at white women and they were considered "colored" by the KKK. It's really weird.

Race and ethnicity are obviously social concepts—they're not biological; they're not genetic things. Like to say "black" people is a really weird generalization. And even more so to say "white" people—does that include Italians or Jews? I'm interested in looking at what and when and where makes someone white and what and when and where makes someone not white or black or whatever. Arabs are the perfect group in which to study those questions, because their place in society is very ambiguous.

Saladin has performed his poetry as a member of Detroit's 1997 National Poetry Slam team. He is also a winner of the 1997 Metro Times Literary Contest.

SERVING THE NEEDS OF THE MULTIETHNIC COMMUNITY
(FOR A SMALL FEE, OF COURSE)

I'm working on my own series of flash cards.

No more

Hellish-images-of-mad-faced-clowns-somersaulting-over-3+3
figures-in-that-traumatic-dance-that-makes-some-kids
forever-avoid-math

Now! Special for mixed babies!
Flash cards of ethnic ambiguity!

And drill time will go something like this . . .

Q: Slightly puffed out hairdo +
   Carhartt jacket +
   Ankh necklace
   that from a distance looks like a
   crucifix =

A: Lessee, that would be—
   "Hey, Holmes,
   give up sum love, Esae!"
   to the tenth power of

homophobic hug withdrawal when
he realizes my name ain't " 'Los"

Q: Hair grown long,
   combed out real straight and
   pulled back in a
   ponytail +
   slight tan
   divided by
   beaded necklace =

A: That one's easy!—
   "Oh, I just loved
   Pocahontas!
   It had such a
   positive message.
   You people are so
   in tune with nature,
   we could've learned so
   much! Too bad we
   killed off nine
   out of ten
   of you."

Q: Deeper tan + hair puffed out even more +
   hoodie multiplied by rolling
   with kids named Anton
   and Kwandoris =

A: Umm . . . I'll guess it's—
   "That boy's gotta be a

quadroon or
something,
trying to pass,
shee-it!"

Q: Month-long growth
of facial hair minus
friendly western voice +
kaffiyeh around neck
to the square root of
crazy look in eyes =

A: Oh, man, I
know this one,
umm . . . —
"He's a greasy,
smelly,
Islamic fundamentalist
terrorist, so we better
search his ass before
he gets on that plane!"

I'm tellin' you,
I'm gonna change the
face
of education.

ARE YOU DATING ME OR MY HAIR?

Dating is this place where all of these issues come to the forefront.
—Monina Diaz, twenty

PEOPLE WANT ME TO CHOOSE

AMANDA HOLZHAUER, sixteen
Cleveland Heights, Ohio
Mother: African-American
Father: European-American (German, Swiss)

I don't date. I don't have time and I'm very picky about my guys. I would never date most of the guys I know to save my soul, but they can be my friends.

It's going to be interesting when I do start dating. People want me to choose. I'm not supposed to want to date white people, I'm not supposed to want to date black people. I don't know what people expect.

I just hope I can find someone who can respect the cultural mix in me and won't think, "You're black, why aren't you dating another black person?" or "You're white, why aren't you dating another white person?"

I LOVE DATING PEOPLE OF ALL RACES

STUART HAY, twenty
Fond du Lac, Wisconsin
Mother: Guyanese (West Indian)
Father: Canadian (Scottish, Irish, French)

I love dating people of all races. I've dated Japanese, Korean, Chinese, mixed girls, and white girls. Now I'm dating an Egyptian girl. My girlfriend and I talk about how beautiful our kids would be. I go out of my way to find somebody who is as different as I am and I love the whole idea of dating someone who is multiracial.

I think that's just my personal bias—mixed people are the most interesting and beautiful people. I'm not going to have a monoracial wife and kids; they're going to be mixed. The idea fascinates me.

I'LL DATE ANYBODY I WANT TO

AYANNA MORIGUCHI, twenty-three
Eugene, Oregon
Mother: Seminole, Scottish, Irish
Father: African-American
Stepfather: African-American

A lot of people have a problem with biracial people dating. If you're black, people expect you to date black guys. But I'll date anybody I want to. I'm mixed. I can date white guys; I can date black guys. And if people say you have to stick with your own race, I can say, "That is my race because I'm white and I'm black."

I lived in Portland for a year. I moved there right after I turned twenty. In Eugene, I'm used to walking around and saying hi to people. But in Portland, they weren't as nice. The girls up there didn't like me because I am light-skinned—that's what people told me. They told me, "The black girls up here don't like mixed girls because the black guys like mixed girls."

The attention from the guys was kind of fun, but I didn't like the negative attention from the females. They wouldn't say anything to me. If I smiled at them, they wouldn't even look at me; they would just walk away. Every black girl in Portland wasn't like that—just a lot of them. It was weird. I always thought we were supposed to stick together.

I DIDN'T FEEL ATTRACTIVE

MEILINA WILKINSON, twenty-one
Farmingdale, New York
Mother: Taiwanese
Father: European-American (English)

I didn't date in high school. I didn't feel attractive. Attractive girls were white and skinny. And I didn't look like that. I didn't look quite white.

I had one friend who was kind of hurtful. After I first met her and told her that I was part Asian, she said, "Oh, don't worry. You can't tell." And she meant that as a compliment.

Most racism in my experience was very subtle, which is just as bad as blatant racism because it feels wrong but you can't put your finger on it. You can't even articulate what you're feeling. The images I saw of Asian women were of women who were submissive, very passive, and eager to please. That's how I think Americans perceive Asian women and I think it's wrong. That's what my friends thought Asian women were like. I couldn't help internalizing that. I didn't have anything else to go by; that's what I saw on TV.

People are now more inclined to say, "Oh, you're part Asian, that's neat" or "You're very exotic-looking." I remember reading this magazine article about how the Eurasian look has started a fire and how it's really pretty fashionable now to be multicultural.

I hope it's not a fad. I hope it's a movement toward more acceptance, because I think the definition of mainstream used to be white, but I think the mainstream now is multicultural. Multiracial, multicultural people are growing in numbers, so people have to accept it now.

219

ARE YOU DATING ME OR MY HAIR?

INDIA,* twenty-three
Indiana
Mother: Native American, Black, White
Father: Native American, Black, White

Most people associate a mixed person with a curly or wavy type of hair texture. I recall this guy I used to date and all he could talk about was my hair. I mean, that's all he would talk about—how long and pretty he thought it was. It got sickening after a while. I started wondering, "Are you dating me or my hair?"

I think sometimes that dating can be more complicated if you're mixed. I would date someone of any race. But then again, I would like to be able to identify with him—to be able to discuss similar problems growing up mixed and have that person say, "Yes, I understand how you feel, that same thing happened to me." Not to say that I couldn't have a discussion like that with a person of a single race. But it would be a little bit easier with someone who's experienced similar situations.

The person who wrestled most deeply with issues about race and dating was Monina Diaz.

WHATEVER PARTNER I CHOOSE SAYS SOMETHING

MONINA DIAZ, twenty
Monrovia, California
Mother: African-American
Father: Puerto Rican

I've been thinking more and more about dating and marriage. These are huge issues for me right now. And no matter what, race will always be a huge issue. Dating is this place where all of these issues come to the forefront.

There are a whole bunch of issues around dating that multiracial individuals deal with. Like who you date can be viewed by other people as reflecting who you align yourself with. People perceive it as making a choice.

When I date a white guy, people look at me like, "She doesn't want to be black, she thinks she's passing." If I date a black guy, from the black community I get, "She's being true, she knows who she is." And if I date a Hispanic guy, it's like, "She's leaning more that way." If I date an Asian guy, it's like, "What's wrong with her? She just wants to forsake everyone." Whatever partner I choose says something.

It's mind-boggling to me that I can date a black man one day and I am like Angela Davis, but if I date an Asian guy the next **221** day, I'm a total sellout. That's just annoying. I hate the fact that no matter who I marry, there will be some message that I'll be sending the world. So I can't make any choice without thinking at some level, even if only subconsciously, "What are people going to think?" "What are people going to say?"

And there have been issues for the people I've dated. I remember I dated this one guy, he was a white guy and he had friends who were Hispanic. He had a house with a pool and so my little brother and my little sister came up and we were all going to go swimming. People would probably identify or categorize my younger sister as a "Mexican girl" without necessarily recognizing her African-American heritage. On the other hand, you can tell that my younger brother is not completely black, but he has very dark skin. So people would probably categorize him as just being black. And then I'm kind of medium-colored.

So I remember this guy and his friends were in shock and I remember hearing them say, "I can't believe that they're brother and sister!" For some of the people I've dated, having kids who look very different from each other would be an issue, even though in my family it's completely normal.

I know for a fact that if I get married and if I have kids I will have no idea what they're going to look like. My older brother is rather dark and his wife is Greek and she has dark hair and olive skin. They had a blond-haired kid with pale skin. He's five years old and he still has blond hair and light skin. Supposedly, my grandmother on my dad's side had blond hair. Of course, we love my nephew, and in our family, there's nothing abnormal about having kids who don't look like us; their next kid may be very dark.

But it was an issue for this one guy to have kids who wouldn't look like him. He said, "All the mixed kids I've seen haven't really

222

looked like their parents." I can see that it would be hard for someone to have a kid who looks nothing like him at all. I could have a kid who's very, very dark, and if I married a white man, he would be saying "son" to this "black" kid. So that might be an issue for someone.

Another issue is that unless I date another multiracial person—there are not a million of them around—he won't understand me completely. Unless I marry a black and Puerto Rican man, there will always be tensions and pressures from society or just issues of not understanding each other. It will always be an interracial relationship and so there will be some lack of being able to relate.

I was joking around with this guy at school. We took this race classification class together. I said, "You know, Brian, we should get married because we're really close friends."

He's a black guy—multiracial black heritage—but considers himself just black. And he goes, "Yeah, but if we get married, our kids are going to be black—none of this one-fourth Puerto Rican stuff."

I said, "No, our kid is going to be part Puerto Rican."

He said, "We could name the kid Enrique—but he's still going to be black."

I laughed, but that's very much the sentiment. Even though he's joking, he just doesn't understand. He knows what the issues are for mixed people because I've talked about them in class and he's studied them, but he doesn't understand deeply.

I don't see myself being able to find someone who will understand these issues. It will be someone who doesn't know what I deal with and doesn't understand it that deeply. That bothers me. But if I find someone I love, I am still going to get married. I am not going to let it stop me from dating who I want. It will be interesting to see who I marry.

223

Many of the people I spoke to said they would prefer to date and marry someone who is also racially mixed. Most of them did not believe that multiracial people are somehow better, more beautiful, or more handsome than other people. But as Monina explained, they suspect that only another racially mixed person can truly "know what I deal with" and "understand deeply." This exemplifies how misunderstood racially mixed people often feel by the larger society.

Although she also feels misunderstood by African-Americans at times, Maya Corey prefers to date black men.

I WILL MARRY AN AFRICAN-AMERICAN

MAYA COREY, nineteen
Minneapolis, Minnesota
Mother: European-American (German)
Father: African

I used to think that the best mate for me would be someone who is biracial like me. That's only because I think a lot of people have stereotypes about mixed-race people—"They're confused," blah, blah, blah. And I've even gotten it from guys I've dated, and it's been annoying. If I do something that seems "too white" or talk a certain way, they'll say, "That must be the white side of you." Sometimes it [being biracial] is supposed to be a positive thing, like, "Oh, you're light-skinned." But that's not cool to me.

It's usually nothing that's too offensive or annoying, it's just the fact that it's there.

I'm pretty sure that I will marry an African-American. They're the ones who are attracted to me and who I'm attracted to. I get a lot more attention from black men. And although I'm ready to challenge the norms in other areas of my life, in that important intimate relationship, I want that person to understand me and vibe with me in as many ways as possible. I personally would not want to deal with all of the issues that come along with being with someone of a different race. It sounds strange coming from me, and it's not that I think it can't be done or that I disagree with it, but it's just something that I don't want to have to deal with. And I'm comfortable with that because I haven't had a lot of attraction to men of other races.

The African-American community is who I am and where I see my children. One thing I'll say about the African-American community is that it's less accepting of interracial relationships. When I was younger and black women saw my mom with me, they were rude. I think the white community is not accepting as well—they just show it in different ways.

But in terms of dealing with biracial kids, every single black family that I've known has been so loving to me and very quick to say, "She's one of ours." I have black friends who I have spent time with on holidays and I've been so comfortable with their families. I see the same sort of family for myself.

"MAYBE IT'S BEST THAT YOU WOULDN'T DATE MY SON"

LESLIE THIBODEAUX, sixteen
Lake Charles, Louisiana
Mother: Creole
Father: Creole

Right now my boyfriend is of white heritage and I've told him the whole history of my family and he accepts it very well. But his mom doesn't. About three months ago, she found out what my heritage is and she called my house and she said, "Maybe it's best that you wouldn't date my son."

I was shocked. She's supposed to have a really strong belief in God and I was quite shocked that she actually had views like that. It really hurt me—it hit really hard when she said that. I was so mad I was shaking.

My boyfriend has no problem with my heritage at all. That is one of the reasons why I truly respect him. Some guys don't know what their friends might say and so they don't date somebody of another race. That was a worry for me. I was like, "What will his friends say and will he treat me differently around them?" But I'm not having any problems with the guy I'm with now. He loves me for who I am on the inside, not just the outside.

After dating for several years, Leslie and her boyfriend broke up. She is now seeing a young man who is also from a Creole family.

* * *

Today, interracial dating is not the huge social taboo that it was for previous generations. According to an October 1997 USA Today/Gallup Poll *survey, 57 percent of polled high school students who date said they had gone out with someone of another race or ethnic group. That's up from just 17 percent of students in a similar poll by Gallup in 1980.*

But many Americans of all racial and ethnic backgrounds still oppose interracial relationships. As a writer for a national magazine that is distributed to teenagers in schools, I've found that interracial dating continues to be a taboo subject in some parts of the country, along with issues like homosexuality and abortion. In the ten years that I've worked on the magazine, we haven't written one full-length feature article about dating across racial lines. Some teachers asked us to steer clear of it for fear that an article would encourage students to date interracially and upset parents and school administrators who oppose it.

WHITE GUYS ASKED THE WHITE GIRLS OUT

CHRISTINE*
African-American and Asian

I always felt ugly. My mom never knew what to do with my hair, so it was huge—I had this big poofy hair. I got teased all the time. A lot of the black girls used relaxers, but at the same time, they didn't like the fact that my hair was long. I remember walking into the bathroom and four girls pulling my hair and running out. It was bad.

In high school, I was in a special program for gifted or talented people. It was a small program; we were really close. But there weren't a lot of black kids in the program. People started dating and the prom got closer and the white guys asked the white girls out. I remember wondering, "What am I going to do for the prom?"

This Swedish exchange student ended up asking me out to the prom. It was actually very cool. He talked about how he thought I was attractive and it really blew my mind.

I remember him coming to my neighborhood. A couple of guys I knew, two black guys, came up to us and they were like, "What you doing with a white man?" And they made fun of him. He felt horrible, embarrassed. Even at my prom—it was a mostly black school—I remember my vice-principal giving me a funny look. Interracial dating was awkward.

One of my ex-boyfriends is Bolivian-American. His parents didn't like the idea of him dating someone who was half black. It was okay if he dated Filipino girls or white girls—anything but black. He told me that his mom started crying when she saw my picture. It's difficult to know that someone can't stand me before they've even met me. It's not a good feeling.

One big concern of mine is that if I ever have kids I'd want them to know that their grandparents love them. I didn't grow up getting to know my own grandparents, my mom's parents, really well. There's always been this tension. It's not talked about, but I know it's there a little bit.

My mom said they had a hard time right after the marriage. Her family didn't talk to her for years and years and years. She said that the first time they met my father, her brother wouldn't even look at him. It was a really difficult experience. I'd hate to have that for my own children. So it makes me wary when I date someone whose parents can't stand me.

I WOULDN'T HAVE BEEN ALLOWED TO DATE HER

KEVIN MAILLARD, twenty-four
Tulsa, Oklahoma
Mother: Black Indian
Father: African-American

There was this organization that I belonged to. I was one of the few people of color in this whole group. We had all of these dorky parties. I never knew who I was going to go with because all of these girls would not want to go with me or they'd make up some lie. After girl seven said no, I was like, "There's a problem here."

My friend said, "Why don't you ask this one girl? She works at the store in the mall. She goes to this school," blah, blah, blah (whisper), "and she's black."

So here I am calling this girl in the middle of nowhere and saying, "Do you want to go to this white-tie formal symphony ball with me?" And of course, that flopped. She was like, "I'm not going to go." That was probably the most awkward experience that I have ever had.

My mother hated those people who tried to pick these girls for me to date. She said, "They cut out so many people that you could have gone out with. I think that's really, really unfortunate."

I dated this same annoying black girl for all of high school. I didn't like her at all. But I didn't have anyone else to go out with. For a really long time, I didn't think of myself as someone who girls would go out with. I'd think, "She probably doesn't think that I'm attractive."

229

I'd be at a party and people would be like, "You have been talking to that girl all night long. Do you like her?"

And I'd be like, "No! Of course not." She would be this beautiful Brooke Shields–type person, and I'd be like, "I don't think she's cute at all," lying half the time.

I wouldn't have been allowed to date her. People looked down on that. It was mainly pressure from friends and also a lot of friends' parents, because in my own family no one looks down upon interracial stuff at all.

It would have been hard to say, "I like this person and nothing's going to stop me and I'm in this all by myself and the world's just going to have to accept it." I think that's really hard. It requires some support.

I wish I had had supportive friends in high school who did not look down on interracial dating and see it as a problem. I wish a friend could have said, "I think you and her would be a nice match," or "Why wouldn't you go out with her? Both of you like soccer, and movies, and alfalfa sprouts." I would have loved to find a group of people like that at home, but I don't think they existed.

"WHY ARE YOU DOING THAT?"

MIRIAM WARREN, sixteen
Las Vegas, Nevada
Mother: European-American (German)
Biological Father: Filipino-American
Adoptive Father: European-American

My boyfriend right now is African-American. I needed someone who is nice and that's just how it ended up. If you date someone outside of your race, people think you are trying to be something that you're not. They say, "Why are you doing that?"

I tell them, "Hey, my boyfriend's the president of the honor society and he studies computer science. He's tall, but he doesn't play basketball, except for fun, and he hasn't been trying to get an athletic scholarship his whole life. He doesn't want to be in the NBA or NFL. He wants to go to an Ivy League school and become a computer scientist or an engineer."

He doesn't fit into their little narrow-minded stereotype. So it makes them feel uncomfortable because the only reason we have stereotypes is because it saves us time. If you stereotype someone, you never have to find out who they really are. You just put them in a box and you don't have to think about it anymore.

THAT WAS THE FIRST TIME
I REALIZED I WAS DIFFERENT

NIKKOLE PALMATIER, twenty-two
Okemos, Michigan
Mother: Japanese
Father: European-American

In the second grade, I had a crush on this white boy. I asked my friend, "Why doesn't he like me?"

My friend said, "It's because you're not white."

That was the first time I had ever heard that. My mental image of myself was that I was just like all my friends. All of my friends were white. I thought I looked just like them. That was the first time I realized I was different and I was literally flabbergasted. I said, "I am too."

She said, "No, you're not."

I actually got in an argument with my friends about it.

"HE DIDN'T THINK YOU WERE ASIAN ENOUGH"

JENNIFER HO, twenty-four
Oakland, California
Mother: European-American (English, French, Irish, Scottish)
Father: Chinese-American

A lot of people are fascinated with Asian culture right now. I've actually been set up on a couple of dates because of this. Someone is like, "He's really into Asian women, you should go out with him." I do. And then afterwards there's always this, "Well, he didn't think you were Asian enough."

It just cracks me up. So they're basically looking for someone to date on the basis of race and not personality, and because of a desire to make themselves one with a culture that's not theirs. They want to be Asian so much, they'll marry into the culture. I feel fortunate not to be the object of their attentions.

I'd like to date people who are Hapa or mixed. There's this need, this desire that I have, to be with someone who is like me, who looks like me. It's this weird sort of biological identification. I just enjoy looking at them. I feel more comfortable around them.

But then I feel that wanting to be with someone on the basis of race is wrong. This kind of thinking—that relationships should be limited to people of a certain race—is exactly what caused people to object to my parents' marriage. And it reminds me of those guys who have to be with a "real" Asian woman—basing a choice on race. I'd like to be color-blind in terms of relationships, because that's how I think the world should be.

233

"EXOTIC" IS HARD TO HEAR

Stefanie is pictured between her brother and sister, Peter and Ursula.

STEFANIE LIANG, nineteen
Newton, Massachusetts
Mother: German-American
Father: Chinese-American

I had a conversation with this guy at a party the other day. He was like, "What's your nationality?"

I said, "I'm American."

And he got annoyed and he said, "Why are you being all PC?"

And I was like, "If you mean my ethnicity, my mother's German and my father is Chinese."

Then he said, "Oh, that's so cool!"

That just really pissed me off and I said, "I don't appreciate you putting a value on my background or you putting me on this unnecessary pedestal for something I have nothing to do with. My background's not what makes me cool."

He said, "But I'm just complimenting you." But actually, I wasn't flattered.

That's the main response I get after I tell people about my background. Instead of saying, "That's interesting. How did your parents meet?" it's like, "Oh, cool!" in this certain tone of voice.

People think I'm attractive or different-looking—kind of unique. They say, "Oh, you're so unique, you're so exotic." I've heard it a million times. When I was younger I thought it was so cool when people called me "exotic." But now I really hate that.

234 It's totally demeaning.

"Exotic" reminds me of the China doll and other weird Asian fetishes. There is often no difference between exotic and erotic to people. So "exotic" is hard to hear, especially from men. After I tell them about my background, I see them looking at me differently and their eyes widening with some erotic and exotic fantasy. I'm always wondering what they're thinking.

I hate the obsession people have with what they see as different or exotic. It's so superficial. It gets to me and I wonder if other mixed people feel that way. I mean, you like the attention, yet you don't. You want people to look at you and it's nice to have people look at you, but sometimes it doesn't feel good to be the only one who's stared at.

It's just another reminder that I'm not like them. It's like they're distancing themselves from me. And no matter what environment I'm in, I'm always going to be the different one. I pride myself on being different but sometimes I don't want to stick out.

People say that mixed people are all beautiful—we've got the "good" hair and the year-round tan. We are beautiful, but not because our parents represent different races. Our beauty is much deeper than that. What's beautiful about us is that we embody harmony and we transcend racism in many ways.

A lot of people view mixed-race people as having a special allure. We represent something different and unusual that many people find exciting and desirable, observes Carla Bradshaw, a clinical psychologist in Seattle, Washington, who is herself biracial. "We have an ambiguous look. We offer what seems like an adventurous and exciting new experience just by our look."

Comments like "You're really exotic-looking" can be flattering. But, Bradshaw notes, "it's a funny kind of compliment. What ex- **235** *actly are people complimenting? It feels like it's about me and not about me at the same time."*

A multiracial person who hears these comments may feel like an object. Jennifer Chau expressed this well in the first chapter of this book. "It can begin to feel like we're mixed-race before we're anything," Bradshaw concludes.

IT'S THE WATERING DOWN OF THE EXOTIC SO IT'S PALATABLE

SARAH ICHIOKA, seventeen
Berkeley, California
Mother: European-American
Father: Japanese-American

In San Francisco newspapers there's a little corner that has the peep-show ads, like "Live Girls" and "Nudie Revues." And one woman's main selling point was that she's mixed Vietnamese and French. I thought it was really interesting.

I was looking through the personal ads, reading the trashy parts of the paper, and I noticed that some guys are looking for "exotic" half-Asian or half-black women. There were an inordinately large number of "Elderly retired white gentleman seeks Oriental companion," over and over and over. Those ads bother me. When people are looking for people of specific races, they're already classifying what they're going to be attracted to. I wouldn't go anywhere near those men.

Like someone told me, "You're so pretty because you're Asian but you have these bright-green eyes." And at the time, I took it as the biggest compliment. I got my eyes from my mom and that's like a bond between us.

But thinking back on it now, I'm like, "So I wouldn't be pretty if I had big brown eyes or big black eyes?" It's like, you wouldn't be beautiful if you were all Asian, but that dab of white in you makes you beautiful. It's the watering down of the exotic so it's palatable. I realize the politics of it now.

237

HAPA GRUB

JEFF YOSHIMI, twenty-eight
Los Angeles, California
Mother: European-American
Father: Japanese-American

Sushi night, Yoshimi style. At the center of the table: a big tray of *gohan* [rice] surrounded by bowls of avocado, cucumber, tuna, crab, chicken salad, sliced Spam, American cheese, etc., etc. There is no bamboo roller in sight, no fancy garnish; there are no little wooden trays. Delicacy is fine, but tonight the family has gathered to pack it in and get stuffed. We pick up our sheets of nori, spread the rice on thick, pile on the goodies, and roll it all up: these, brothers and sisters, are Hapa burritos.

I look around the dinner table. My sister takes the conservative single-ingredient approach. She makes cucumber rolls, crab rolls—taquitos, I guess—and dips them into the soy sauce.

My mom doesn't roll so well, and she likes to put in one of everything, so that her first bite (and you should see the look on her face when she takes that first bite!) sends half her filling crashing on the plate.

Me and my dad, we've got the system—crab, avocado, and a healthy squirt of that squeeze-bottle mayonnaise, rolled up tight and chased with a cold hit of Asahi Dry [a Japanese beer]. Then a chicken salad and cheese, and finally a straight-up Spam roll.

So there you have it. Sushi, one of the great symbols of Japan, the tourist's fear and yuppie's pride, living large on our dining room table.

"But wait!" somebody yells. "Is that really sushi? Is that Japanese, or is it some kind of American mutation of sushi? Is that meal you're raving about American?"

Well . . . no, not exactly. I mean, it's a far cry from meat and potatoes with a glass of milk. (Milk and sushi? Gross!)

"Well, then, I'm confused, what the hell *is* that? It's not Japanese, it's not American—man, there's no way to name it, Jeff, and I'm all mixed up."

Yah, buddy, *you're* confused, *you're* mixed up. I'm just Hapa, proud, and feeling fat after some good down-home grub.

Food—like language, music, religion, and dance—is an expression of culture. It is mundane and unglamorous, but absolutely essential to life. And indeed, whether we realize it or not, food is often a part of our cultural and ethnic identity. When I reminisce about the old Zojirushi rice cooker—blowing up its trail of steam and popping with a springlike click from red "rice cooking" to orange "keep warm"—and the person I'm talking to laughs and says, "Yah, I remember, and wasn't it nasty when you forgot about that rice and three days later it was all brown and form-fitted to the bottom of the cooker," then I know that that person shares something with me. He or she grew up with *gohan,* and in this seemingly minor but actually significant way, we both know what it means to be Japanese.

Or perhaps you, the reader, laughed to yourself when you read the word *Spam* at the top of the page. Spam, that funky pink gelatinous mystery that tastes so good with fried eggs. Why do you and I both laugh at it? Probably because you and I both ate it, or were scared of it, growing up. We're both American.

Rice—Japanese; Spam—American. Two foods, two cultures, a nice little dichotomy that is easy to remember and even easier to impose. East and West with all middles excluded, for "never the twain shall meet." Convenient, to be sure, but in our changing world, problematic. What, after all, are we to do with the Spam-sushi burrito? Well, I can tell you what *I* do with it. I eat it, bite by glorious bite, happy as can be, and: Surprise! Nowhere in my mouth do Spam and rice flee to their respective cultural repositories. They are at peace, internally coherent, unconfused, and utterly delicious.

True, this "sushi" is composed of elements that can be traced to separate cultures. The rice and seaweed are from Japan; the Spam is America's claim to fame. (And what of the burrito format, of what lineage is that?) So my meal is at least bicultural, if not tricultural or polycultural. But it is at the same time a unity, a single innovation of multiple descent.

What can be said of Hapa eats can be said of Hapa eaters. We don't fit nicely into any of the standard cultural categories, but we don't deny those cultures either. Instead we are a new culture, with a new way of seeing the world, a new language (you should hear how I say *nori*), and even new foods, all of which reflect our diverse heritage. Our example has been silly, but it is a real example, indicative of my experiences not only as a Hapa eater, but as a Hapa in general.

For me, being Hapa has always been gratifying, a source of pride. And I am an optimist. I think that, given the right conditions, other facets of culture and life, and other cultures altogether, can follow the model of the Spam-sushi burrito. In fact, they already have. Tex-Mex, pidgin Hawaiian, Aram sandwiches*—these phenomena didn't just pop up out of nowhere, they have roots as diverse as their names, but for the most part we accept them and appreciate them on their own terms, without giving their existence a second thought.

The way I see it, America at the close of the twentieth century and beyond is not a vast melting pot of assimilation, but a transient mosaic—a kaleidoscope—whose individual colors and patterns reconfigure from generation to generation and are never lost, but are constantly found anew.

This is the first of a series of "Hapa Grub" columns that Jeff wrote for What's Hapa'ning: The Hapa Issues Forum Newsletter. *It was published in fall 1993.*

---

*Sandwiches sold in some Middle Eastern restaurants in Berkeley, California. The author defines an Aram sandwich as lettuce, tomato, and cheese stuffed into pitalike bread that is rolled up like a burrito.

DOUBLE-BREED

I've heard biracial people use the term double-breed *to describe themselves. Rather than view themselves as "half," or less than whole, they see themselves as "double," or in the case of multiracial people who have three or four heritages, perhaps "triple" or "quadruple."*

Many of the people I interviewed for this book talked about the positives of being racially mixed. Here are some of the highlights.

I'M TWO FLAVORS

MIRIAM WARREN, sixteen
Las Vegas, Nevada
Mother: European-American (German)
Biological Father: Filipino-American
Adoptive Father: European-American

Being biracial, you endure a little more hardship because you hear all of these "What are you?" questions and you question yourself more. But that makes you a more open-minded person.

I think that biracial people, on the whole, are nonconformists. They break the mold. They do things that are a little bit out of the ordinary and they are not afraid to say, "Hey, this cultural genre just doesn't work," or "This little box that we put ourselves into just isn't right, and just because everyone's doing it doesn't make it acceptable."

I put myself out on a limb. People say I'm a little too controversial or a little too outspoken. But in the end, the rewards that I reap are just astounding. All the things that I have done so far in only sixteen years impress a lot of people who are much older than I am. And if I could snap my fingers today and become a white girl or a Filipino girl, I wouldn't do it.

I like to call myself "ice cream with sprinkles," because everyone can have just one flavor—I'm two flavors. And that makes me even cooler—just a little more colorful.

WE'RE OPEN TO . . .
DIFFERENT EXPERIENCES

SALADIN ALI AHMED, twenty-two
Dearborn, Michigan
Mother: European-American (Irish)
Stepmother: European-American
Father: Arab-American

I don't think mixed-race people are special or better than anybody else. But sometimes I think we're in a position to view the world with more open eyes, with more references to pull on. We're open to a lot of different experiences, a lot of different influences. We tend to hang with a bigger variety of people. Our cultural influences—like the music that we listen to—are probably broader.

Being mixed-race can be a confusing and weird experience sometimes. You have more stuff to learn about yourself than other people do, but that's a good thing. And you have more stuff to teach other people.

15

YOU CAN LOOK AT THINGS A LITTLE MORE DEEPLY

BRIAN HARRIS, sixteen
Stanton, California
Mother: European-American
Father: African-American

Being biracial makes you a little more understanding about a lot of things, especially if you're black and white, because you're on both sides of a huge racial divide. You can look at things a little more deeply than other people might.

Like blacks and whites had two completely different feelings about the O. J. Simpson trial, and if you were a member of both groups, you were in an odd position. And with the Rodney King beating—there were black people feeling one way and white people feeling another way, and you were kind of in the middle.

Sometimes there's a reason for people to be suspicious about law enforcement. After seeing what you feel to be unfair—justice not being blind to color, harsher sentences for black people—you start to not trust the system. The people who feel like they're getting their fair shot at justice are less likely to question a verdict.

I try to bring up people's level of understanding and knowledge of each other to eliminate some of the ignorance. I've spoken at a lot of different junior high and high schools for the Orange County Human Rights Commission. I talk about being biracial and about racism and stereotypes. I've spoken at teachers' colleges about multiculturalism and about what teachers can do to help their students be more tolerant of each other.

246

In Friendship Sees No Color [the pen-pal club described in the chapter Check One Box], I try to give people an opportunity to write to somebody of a different race and maybe disprove some of their own stereotypes, because you are less likely to hate people when you think they might have a lot in common with you. Just making one person a little more educated is making progress.

IT WAS MY JOB TO BE A BRIDGE

ERIC KOJI STOWE, twenty-six
Sacramento, California
Mother: Japanese-American
Father: African-American

I don't segregate myself from everyone else by totally jumping into a certain group. An example would be that a lot of my friends in the African-American community are really tight and I'm close to them, but I won't let myself hang out solely with that group of people. I never want to limit myself to a certain group of friends or people; I always want to keep myself really open.

In high school, I played football, so I hung out with the football players, who were pretty much African-American, and I felt really comfortable in that social setting. And in the classrooms, since I took college prep classes, there were hardly any African-Americans. So I felt fairly comfortable hanging out among whites.

I had six really close friends; half of them were white and half of them were African-American. They never hung out together. It felt like it was my job to be a bridge between my white friends and my black friends.

Once I got to college, which was [University of California] **247**

Davis, it was pretty much the epitome of higher learning, where everyone was really separated and there were very few African-Americans. So we had a really close tight-knit group. But all of my roommates ended up being Asian.

My African-American friends and my Asian friends didn't really communicate. I was again that bridge between the two. I tried to get rid of the stereotypes they had about each other and mediate or ease the tension. If it wasn't for myself and my peers who are biracial, the two groups would probably have never gotten along.

IT GIVES ME A BENEFIT OF SYNTHESIS

BRIAN COLWELL, twenty-three
Cupertino, California
Mother: Japanese-American
Father: European-American

Instead of thinking of myself as being half something and a part of something else, I think of myself as having a double heritage. Being mixed-race, you get this merging of two cultural perspectives and cultural experiences—the people you meet, the things you do, the places you might go. You can sort through them and compare them and take what you want.

Anytime you have synthesis like that, it's a good thing—whether it's in the sciences, or in nature, or in social situations. I'm saying synthesis as opposed to having two parts that are fighting with each other. Sometimes there's conflict too. But in general, these two parts come together and form something new, which is different from either part and incorporates elements of both. It makes a unified strong single from the two.

The other thing about being mixed-race is that you're exposed to two different families. My mother and my father are like the sun and the moon. My mother's family is quiet and reserved. My mother and her father are hard working and have a very strong work ethic. On my father's side it's more "do your thing." My father's family is very warm and social. The dynamics are different.

Being able to look to the left and see my mom's family and look to the right and see my father's family exposes me to two totally different types of structures in terms of family, types of people, behavior, attitudes, and everything. That also gives me a benefit of synthesis.

I feel that being exposed to two drastically different alternatives and being exposed to more input, more of the world, has made me stronger.

It's made me think twice before I give anybody a problem because of the way they look—because of their ethnicity, or their height, or their sex, or their age, or anything else. It brings a different sensitivity to my outlook on the world. I don't know what I'd do if I were without it. I love it.

YOU BECOME MORE ADEPT AT FINDING OUT WHO YOU ARE

MITZI UEHARA CARTER, twenty-three
Houston, Texas
Mother: Japanese-American (Okinawan)
Father: African-American

I think I've explored myself a lot more than other people my age, as far as identity choices go. Being mixed, you have to search for an identity faster. A lot of times it can cause stress, but in the end it makes you a stronger person. Psychologically, you become more adept at finding out who you are. You've already done this groundwork of trying to figure yourself out.

I was trying to explain this to a guy on a plane back from La Paz, Bolivia. He told me that his brother adopted a black girl and they lived in a white neighborhood and she was having a really hard time. And he said, "I would never do that to any child." Then he went on about biracial people. He said, "Children have a hard enough life. Why add the stress of being biracial? Why do that to a child?"

I said, "You know, I love it and I'm really glad that I am biracial because I've learned so much from it." You have a unique outlook on the world. It gives you a third lens not many others have, especially if you've been raised to learn and appreciate your ethnic heritages.

Today, I think it's easier to be biracial because people are more **250** accepting of mixed-race people. In California, I get the feeling that it's the cool thing now to be interracial or biracial. I'm very proud of it.

However, I'm somewhat wary of biracial people being exoticized and portrayed in the media as the answer to racism and other troubling issues. I don't want to be labeled as the nouveau wonder recipe—"mix and you'll end racism."

WE'RE BLENDERS

STUART HAY, twenty
Fond du Lac, Wisconsin
Mother: Guyanese (West Indian)
Father: Canadian (Scottish, Irish, French)

Some people look at being biracial as a problem. I see it as being blessed. I see it as an advantage in every way. As more immigrants come to this country and we become a more diverse society, I think multiracial people will have an advantage in being able to cross over racial boundaries with greater ease than people who are designated in certain distinct, separate groups.

Multiracial people can relate to maybe three cultures instead of being stuck in one group and seeing everyone else as being out-groups and out-members. We're able to cross over because we do it in our own families. We're blenders.

It comes down to each individual and how you were raised. If you grow up in a good family, and they instill good values in you and tell you not to be afraid of what other people think, it's a strengthening experience. It makes you a strong person if you can define yourself and not let anyone else define you.

251

Being biracial, you do examine yourself a lot. You wonder a lot of times when you're with one group, "Is this the group that I belong in? I can get along with them, but they don't like this part of my culture, so do I fully belong with these people?" Then you go to other people. You find pluses and minuses with both groups.

Eventually, you can either learn to manage it or you can have trouble with it. And I feel like I've learned to manage being who I am and I enjoy different cultures and different people. I think it's beneficial and strengthening.

RESOURCES

In the past, multiracial people were such a small group and so widely scattered that finding others to connect with could be a daunting task. But today, no matter where you live, you can join a lively discussion with multiracial people in a cyberspace chat room or attend a conference organized by a mixed-race student group at a nearby college.

As the number of interracial families and racially mixed people has grown, so has the number of associations, books, Web sites, films, and other resources for and about them. I've listed some of the most interesting and informative resources in this chapter. They cover a wide variety of issues and target varied audiences, including teens, parents of mixed-race children, college students, teachers, and counselors.

Some Web site addresses may have changed since the publication of this book. So if a site fails to come up, you can probably find it by plugging the name of the group into a search engine.

AFFINITY AND ADVOCACY GROUPS

ASSOCIATION OF MULTIETHNIC AMERICANS (AMEA)
Web site: www.ameasite.org
E-mail: ameapres@aol.com
AMEA was formed in November 1988 as the first national umbrella group for multiracial/ethnic Americans and their families. AMEA's primary goal is to promote a positive awareness of interracial and multiethnic identity. AMEA was the first multiracial/ethnic organization to be appointed to the federal 2000 Census Advisory Committee in Washington, D.C., in 1995. The AMEA Web site has information about social groups around the country for multiracial families and individuals, legislative policy issues, medical issues, and much more.

FAMLEE HOMEPAGE
Web site: www.sccs.swarthmore.edu/~thompson/famlee/home.html
Famlee is a group of over one hundred people celebrating multiculturalism and multiraciality. Most of its members are mixed-race young adults in the United States. The

Famlee listserv is a lively forum where issues such as dating, 2000 census racial categories, Puerto Rican history, and Creole culture have been discussed.

HAPA ISSUES FORUM (HIF)
Web site: www.hapaissuesforum.org
Founded in 1992 by multiracial students at the University of California at Berkeley, HIF is one of the largest nonprofit organizations addressing issues of mixed heritage. HIF focuses on the role that mixed-race Asians play in the Asian-American community and in our multicultural society. HIF sponsors an annual conference, publishes a quarterly newsletter, holds social and cultural activities, and has an e-mail discussion group. HIF has chapters in Berkeley, Santa Barbara, and Los Angeles, but its membership is worldwide.

INTERRACIAL INDIVIDUALS DISCUSSION LIST (II-LIST)
Web site: www.geocities.com/Wellesley/6426/ii.html
II-List is an interracial issues listserv that boasts about one hundred members of all ages who primarily live in the United States. This list is described as a place where racially mixed people can share experiences, vent frustrations, and ask questions without being bashed by insensitive and ignorant people.

MY SHOES
Web site: http://myshoes.com
This site is billed as a support group in cyberspace hosted by clinical psychologist Dr. Juanita Brooks. It is primarily for biracial/multiracial children, adolescents, and adults who have a white appearance and wish to interact with others of similar heritage. There are two support groups—one for children and teens and one for adults.

PROJECT RACE—RECLASSIFY ALL CHILDREN EQUALLY, INC.
Web site: http://projectrace.home.mindspring.com
E-mail: ProjRACE@aol.com
Project RACE is a national organization that advocates for multiracial children and adults through education, community awareness, and legislation: "Our main goal is for a multiracial classification on all school, employment, state, federal, local, census, and medical forms requiring racial data."

AMERASIAN ADVOCACY

AMERASIAN NETWORK
Web site: www.amerasian.org
A nonprofit organization that operates in Vietnam to benefit Amerasians and other displaced young people.

THE FILIPINO AMERICAN MOVEMENT FOR AMERASIAN SERVICES (FAMAS)
Web site: www.famas.org/famas.htm
Hundreds of thousands of Amerasian children who were fathered by U.S. servicemen in Asia were left behind by their fathers. There are about 50,000 Amerasian children in the Philippines (this only includes those born between 1987 and 1992). These pages promote FAMAS, which is working to reunite these children with their fathers and pass legislation to allow entry and immigration of these children to the United States.

INTERRACIAL COUPLES

INTERRACE HAVEN
Web site: www.eden.com/~crusader/irhaven.html
This site was created as a source of information, resources, and support for people who are in interracial relationships, biracial and multiracial individuals, parents and grandparents of a biracial or multiracial child, and anyone interested in being supportive to one or all of the above. It includes a picture gallery of interracial couples, a chat room, and links to related sites.

INTERRACIAL
Web site: www.twsonline.com/INTERracial
The creators of this site hope to bring about acceptance of and offer support for interracial/intercultural couples and biracial/multicultural children. It includes various articles and chat forums. There is a chat room and discussion forum exclusively for people under eighteen.

MAGAZINES AND E-ZINES

INTERRACE
P.O. Box 17479
Beverly Hills, CA 90209
Web site: http://members.aol.com/intrace/index.html
A print magazine for and about interracial couples, families, singles, and multiracial people. *Interrace* also offers interracial books and products for sale, personal ads for singles, an interracial living guide, and an annual cruise. *Interrace* is published four times a year and is available by subscription and at select bookstores and newsstands nationwide.

INTERRACIAL VOICE
P.O. Box 560185
College Point, NY 11356-0185
E-mail: intvoice@webcom.com
Web site: www.webcom.com/~intvoice
Interracial Voice is an e-zine published every other month at the Web site above. It is described as an independent, information-oriented networking news journal, serving the mixed-race/interracial community in cyberspace, with the goal of universal recognition of mixed-race individuals as constituting a separate "racial" entity. Includes a large collection of articles, essays, and poems by various authors, announcements of mixed-race events around the country, requests for help from researchers, Interracial Voice On-line Bookstore, and lots of links to other sites.

MAVIN: THE ARTICULATE JOURNAL OF THE MIXED-RACE EXPERIENCE
1102 Eighth Ave., #407
Seattle, WA 98101
E-mail: mavin@aa.net
Web site: www.mavin.net
A quarterly magazine, staffed by college students, that is dedicated to the celebration of the mixed-race experience in America; a resource for mixed-race individuals

RESOURCES

and organizations on college campuses across the country. While *Mavin* itself is geared toward adults and college students, there are plans to include a newsletter aimed at middle school and high school students. *Mavin* also has a listserv.

MÉTISSE MAGAZINE
Web site: www.metisse.com
An on-line magazine dedicated to providing a forum for multicultural and multiracial women in cyberspace. The French word *métisse* describes a woman who is multicultural or multiracial. The site features a famous *métisse* woman each month and has a discussion forum.

BOOKS

An asterisk (*) before a title indicates that children or teens may have difficulty reading this book because of its subject matter and/or language level.

YOUNG ADULT, NONFICTION

BLACK INDIANS: A HIDDEN HERITAGE
William Loren Katz (Aladdin Paperbacks, 1997; Ethrac Publications, 1986)
A history of the relationship between African-Americans and American Indians, including the Black Indians, from the early colonization of the Americas.

DIFFERENT WORLDS: INTERRACIAL AND CROSS-CULTURAL DATING
Janet Bode and Iris Rosoff (Franklin Watts, 1989)
Teenagers who are involved in interracial relationships talk about peer pressure, the reactions of parents, and other issues.

FORBIDDEN LOVE: THE SECRET HISTORY OF MIXED-RACE AMERICA
Gary Nash (Henry Holt, 1999)
A historian excavates the buried history of racially mixed people in the United States from the time of John Rolfe and Pocahontas to Tiger Woods. He uses stories, paintings, and biographies to bring this history to life.

"I AM WHO I AM": SPEAKING OUT ABOUT MULTIRACIAL IDENTITY
Kathlyn Gay (Franklin Watts, 1995)
Based on interviews with teenagers and experts, this book gives readers a positive yet realistic look at the experiences of racially mixed young people.

MEMOIRS AND BIOGRAPHIES

BLACK, WHITE, OTHER: BIRACIAL AMERICANS TALK ABOUT RACE AND IDENTITY
Lise Funderburg (Quill, 1995)
A powerful collection of forty-six interviews with racially mixed adults of primarily white and black heritage. The author is biracial.

257

THE COLOR OF WATER: A BLACK MAN'S TRIBUTE TO HIS WHITE MOTHER
James McBride (Riverhead Books, 1997)
The true story of a biracial man who grew up in Brooklyn's Red Hook projects and his mother, a Jewish woman who married a black man.

COMPOSITION IN BLACK AND WHITE: THE LIFE OF PHILIPPA SCHUYLER
Kathryn Talalay (Oxford University Press, 1995; reprinted in 1997)
The story of Philippa Schuyler, a biracial child prodigy in the 1930s, and later a concert pianist, composer, and journalist, highlights the overwhelming burdens that are sometimes placed on multiracial people by their parents and society.

FREEDOM'S CHILD: THE LIFE OF A CONFEDERATE GENERAL'S BLACK DAUGHTER
Carrie Allen McCray (Algonquin, 1998)
McCray writes a biography about her mother, Mary Rice Hayes Allen, who was the daughter of General J. R. Jones of the Confederate Army and Malinda Rice, a black servant girl. Mary, who was acknowledged by Jones as his daughter, became a fighter for civil rights.

LIFE ON THE COLOR LINE: THE TRUE STORY OF A WHITE BOY WHO DISCOVERED HE WAS BLACK
Gregory Williams (Plume, 1996)
Williams, who grew up thinking he was white, writes about the dramatic changes that take place in his life, identity, and worldview after his parents split up and he is taken to live with his father's impoverished black family.

ON GOLD MOUNTAIN: THE ONE-HUNDRED-YEAR ODYSSEY OF A CHINESE-AMERICAN FAMILY
Lisa See (Vintage, 1996)
The author presents a portrait of her Chinese-American family, starting with her great-grandfather who immigrated to the United States from China, married a white woman, and became a successful businessman in Los Angeles.

SLAVES IN THE FAMILY
Edward Ball (Farrar, Straus & Giroux, Inc., 1998)
On their twenty plantations in South Carolina, the author's ancestors enslaved close to 4,000 Africans and African-Americans. Ball grapples with his family's slaveholding past and tracks down the descendants of Ball slaves. He meets African-Americans who are long-lost relatives.

THE SWEETER THE JUICE: A FAMILY MEMOIR IN BLACK AND WHITE
Shirlee Taylor Haizlip (Touchstone, 1995)
Going back six generations, Haizlip traces the lives of her relatives—those who lived as blacks and those who assimilated into white society.

HISTORY/SOCIAL ISSUES

**AMERICAN MIXED RACE: THE CULTURE OF MICRODIVERSITY*
Naomi Zack, editor (Rowman & Littlefield Publishers, Inc., 1995)
A collection of twenty-two essays, studies, and research papers addressing the mixed-race experience, covering autobiography, art, social science, public policy, and identity theory. Many contributors are racially mixed.

**AMERICAS: THE CHANGING FACE OF LATIN AMERICA AND THE CARIBBEAN*
Peter Winn (University of California Press, 1995)

A history of Latin America and the Caribbean covering historical, demographic, political, social, cultural, religious, and economic trends.

EMBRACING THE STRANGER: INTERMARRIAGE AND THE FUTURE OF THE AMERICAN JEWISH COMMUNITY
Ellen Jaffe McClain (HarperCollins, 1995)
Through interviews with intermarried couples and Jewish community leaders, the author highlights the renewed vitality of faith in many of these unions and calls for better treatment of intermarried couples by the Jewish community.

HALF AND HALF: WRITERS ON GROWING UP BIRACIAL AND BICULTURAL
Claudine C. O'Hearn, editor (Pantheon Books, 1998)
O'Hearn presents a collection of personal essays by some of the most interesting and important writers on the experience of being biracial and bicultural in the United States today.

LOVE'S REVOLUTION: RACIAL INTERMARRIAGE
Maria P. P. Root (Temple University Press, 1999)
This book is based on Root's five-year study of 200 interracial families around the country. Root uses interracial marriage as a vehicle for exploring race in America. The book is filled with excerpts of interviews she conducted with interracially married people, their children, their parents, and others.

*MIXED BLOOD: INTERMARRIAGE AND ETHNIC IDENTITY IN TWENTIETH-CENTURY AMERICA
Paul R. Spickard (University of Wisconsin Press, 1991)
The author analyzes the experiences of people in intermarriage as a function of social structural factors, such as demographics, as well as the images that people have of other ethnic groups and of themselves.

MIXED MATCHES: HOW TO CREATE SUCCESSFUL INTERRACIAL, INTERETHNIC, AND INTERFAITH MARRIAGES
Joel Crohn (Fawcett Book Group, 1995)
Written by a therapist, this self-help book discusses the strains that can arise between people in an interracial or any other type of "mixed" relationship. Exercises are given to help readers identify and resolve their issues.

*THE MULTIRACIAL EXPERIENCE: RACIAL BORDERS AS THE NEW FRONTIER
Maria P. P. Root, editor (Sage Publications, 1996)
E-mail: order@sagepub.com
In this second of two groundbreaking volumes, Root pulls together research studies and writings about the American mixed-race experience. Most of the contributors are racially mixed. (See below, *Racially Mixed People in America*.)

*MULTIRACIAL IDENTITY AND THE NEW MILLENNIUM: BLACK NO MORE OR MORE THAN BLACK?
G. Reginald Daniel (Temple University Press, 1999)
This book examines the impact that contemporary multiracial identity may have on how blackness is defined in the United States in the twenty-first century and beyond.

*NEW PEOPLE: MISCEGENATION AND MULATTOES IN THE UNITED STATES
Joel Williamson (Louisiana State University Press, 1995)
How has miscegenation influenced our national culture? In this book Williamson traces contact between whites and blacks from the inception of the United States to the present time, including the "new people" created by interracial relationships.

RACE AND MIXED RACE
Naomi Zack (Temple University Press, 1993; reprinted in 1995)
Zack explores the historical, social, and philosophical problems resulting from how race is defined in the United States.

RACIALLY MIXED PEOPLE IN AMERICA
Maria P. P. Root, editor (Sage Publications, 1992)
Root brings together research studies and writings by educators, sociologists, social workers, philosophers, and others on the American mixed-race experience. Most of the contributors are racially mixed or the parents of mixed-race children.

RECONFIGURING RACE, RE-ARTICULATING ETHNICITY: MULTIRACIAL IDENTITY AND ASIAN AMERICA
Teresa Kay Williams and Cynthia Nakashima, editors (Temple University Press, 1999)
A collection of articles written about racially mixed people of Asian descent in the United States and in other parts of the world.

VIETNAMERICA: THE WAR COMES HOME
Thomas Bass (Soho Press, 1997)
In Vietnam, the Amerasian children of U.S. servicemen are called "the dust of life." This book describes the lives of Amerasians abandoned by their fathers and ostracized by the Vietnamese.

WHITE BY DEFINITION: SOCIAL CLASSIFICATION IN CREOLE LOUISIANA
Virginia R. Dominguez (Rutgers University Press, 1994)
Based on a study of the ethnic identity of Louisiana Creoles, the book discusses how race and racial categories are defined and maintained.

ADULT, FICTION

CAUCASIA
Danzy Senna (Putnam, 1998)
Growing up in an interracial family in Boston in the 1970s, Birdie's life changes when her family falls apart and her father and darker-skinned sister move to Brazil. After living in New Hampshire with her white mother, where she endures the racism of whites, she runs away to find her father and sister.

HOUSE OF WAITING
Marina Budhos (Global Cities, 1995)
A young woman flees her Orthodox Jewish home to marry an Indo-Caribbean man.

A LITTLE TOO MUCH IS ENOUGH
Kathleen Tyau (Norton Paperback, 1996)
The coming-of-age story of Mahealani Wong, a teenager growing up in a multicultural Chinese-Hawaiian family in Hawaii in the 1950s.

THE WEDDING
Dorothy West (Anchor, 1996)
Set in an elite African-American community on Martha's Vineyard in the 1950s, this novel explores the meaning of race and class in one multiracial African-American family.

A YELLOW RAFT IN BLUE WATER
Michael Dorris (Warner Books, 1988)
The author weaves together the stories of three women—Rayona, who is part black, and her Native American mother and grandmother.

YOUNG ADULT, FICTION

ARILLA SUN DOWN
Virginia Hamilton (Scholastic Professional Books, 1995)
Struggling for a sense of identity as African-American and Native American, Arilla Adams is unable to identify with a single race.

JUBILEE JOURNEY
Carolyn Meyer (Harcourt Brace Children's Books, 1997)
Emily Rose Chartier, a biracial thirteen-year-old, explores how racism affected three generations of her family.

THE LAST RAINMAKER
Sherry Garland (Harcourt Brace Children's Books, 1997)
In this story set in the late 1800s, thirteen-year-old Caroline, who was raised to believe her late Native American mother was Italian, discovers the truth about her dual heritage.

MEMORIES OF MY GHOST BROTHER
Heinz Insu Fenkl (Dutton Books, 1996)
A young Amerasian man searches for his true identity.

SONG OF THE BUFFALO BOY (GREAT EPISODES)
Sherry Garland (Harcourt Brace Jovanovich, 1994)
Loi's family promises to wed her to an older man, so the seventeen-year-old flees to Ho Chi Minh City and, with her buffalo-herding boyfriend, prepares to leave for America in search of her biological father.

MOVIES AND VIDEOS

These videos are a resource for teachers and organizations. At the time this book was published, rental costs averaged $60, and purchase prices ranged from $125 to $445.

A CULTURE IN COMMON
Producer: Regge Life
1997, 30 minutes
A shorter version of *Doubles,* which is suitable for children junior high to college.
Distributed by:
Film Ideas, Inc.
308 North Wolf Rd.
Wheeling, IL 60090
E-mail: Filmid@ais.net
Web site: www.filmideas.com

DOUBLES: JAPAN AND AMERICA'S INTERCULTURAL CHILDREN
Producer: Regge Life
1995, 90 minutes
After World War II, thousands of children were born to Japanese women and American servicemen. Some left Japan, but others were abandoned by their parents. What has life been like for them in Japan? In America? To answer these questions, a number of these intercultural people are interviewed in this film. The title, *Doubles,* is the word some of them use to describe themselves, as opposed to *half.*
To rent or buy (schools only):
Doubles Project
22D Hollywood Ave.
Ho-Ho-Kus, NJ 07423
E-mail: TMCNDY@aol.com

Contact Filmakers Library to buy or rent the next four films at:
124 East 40th Street, Suite 901
New York, NY 10016
E-mail: info@filmakers.com
Web site: www.filmakers.com

BETWEEN BLACK AND WHITE
Producer: Giannella Garrett
1994, 26 minutes
Four people of black and white parentage are featured. Each is identified by society as black or white, but rarely as both. The film asks whether the racial categories "black" and "white" are relevant.

JUST BLACK?: MULTIRACIAL IDENTITY
Producers: Francine Winddance Twine, Jonathan F. Warren, and Francisco Ferrandiz
1992, 57 minutes
Twine, an anthropologist, interviews several college students of mixed descent about family relationships, dating, friendship, and their childhood experiences. Each has one black parent and a white, Asian, or Hispanic second parent. The students share their struggles to establish and assert a racial identity.

NONE OF THE ABOVE
Director: Erika Surat Anderson
1994, 23 minutes
Anderson, a mixed-race person of (Asian) Indian and Danish-American descent, describes her own search for identity and community and interviews several other multiracial people.

SEOUL II SOUL
Director: Hak J. Chung
1999, 25 minutes
The film takes viewers into the home of an African-American veteran of the Korean War, his Korean wife, and their three grown children.

Contact the National Asian American Telecommunications Association (NAATA) for purchase or rental of the following movies. There is also an option to view the movies for $15 before deciding to rent or buy. Most of the descriptions below were taken from the NAATA catalogue.

NAATA/Cross Current Media
346 Ninth St., 2nd Fl.
San Francisco, CA 94103
Web site: www.naatanet.org

BANANA SPLIT
Producer/Director: Kip Fulbeck
1990, 37 minutes
This video explores identity and biracial ethnicity issues, focusing on Fulbeck's parents' relationship with each other and their respective acclamations and rejections of each other's cultures. It also addresses ethnic dating patterns and stereotypes.

DAYS OF WAITING
Producer/Director: Steven Okazaki
1988, 28 minutes
Academy Award Winner, Best Documentary Short Subject
Artist Estelle Ishigo was one of the few Caucasians interned with 100,000 Japanese-Americans in 1942 because she refused to be separated from her Japanese-American husband. The sketches and paintings she produced over four years in the Heart Mountain Camp in Wyoming portray life behind the barbed wire.

DO TWO HALVES REALLY MAKE A WHOLE?
Producer/Director: Martha Chono-Helsley
1993, 30 minutes
This video features the diverse viewpoints of people with multiracial Asian heritages, including African- and Japanese-American poet and playwright Velina Hasu Houston and Chinese-Japanese Chicana-Scots storyteller, actress, and performance artist Brenda Wong Aoki.

QUIET PASSAGES: THE JAPANESE AMERICAN WAR BRIDE EXPERIENCE
Director: Tim DePaepe
Producers: Chico Herbison and Jerry Schultz
1991, 26 minutes, with study guide
The lives of thousands of Japanese women were transformed during the Occupation when they met and married American servicemen, defying custom and law. Through interviews with their children, and personal and archival photos and footage, this film follows the journey of several of these women to the Midwest.

THE STORY OF VINH
Producer/Director: Keiko Tsuno
1990, 60 minutes
The son of a U.S. serviceman and a Vietnamese woman arrives in New York City, dazed and confused, speaking no English. Through his eyes, we are compelled to examine the complex legacy of abandoned children during wartime.

INTERRACIAL FAMILY ORGANIZATIONS

There are more than forty organizations across the country that provide support, resources, and activities for interracial and multicultural individuals and families. Some of the largest and longest-running groups are listed below. The AMEA Web site (see first page of this resource guide) lists the locations of other groups.

BIRACIAL FAMILY NETWORK
P.O. Box 3214
Chicago, IL 60654
E-mail: http://bfnnewsltr@aol.com

GIFT (GETTING INTERRACIAL/INTERCULTURAL FAMILIES TOGETHER)
P.O. Box 1281
Montclair, NJ 07042
E-mail: NJGIFT@aol.com
Web site: http://members.aol.com/njgift/index.html

HONOR OUR NEW ETHNIC YOUTH (HONEY)
P.O. Box 23241
Eugene, OR 97402

INTERRACIAL FAMILY AND SOCIAL ALLIANCE
P.O. Box 35109
Dallas, TX 75235-0109
Web site: www.flash.net/~mata9/ifsa.htm

THE INTERRACIAL FAMILY CIRCLE
P.O. Box 53291
Washington, D.C. 20009
E-mail: ifcweb@hotmail.com
Web site: www.geocities.com/Heartland/Estates/4496/

INTERRACIAL-INTERCULTURAL PRIDE (I-PRIDE)
P.O. Box 11811
Berkeley, CA 94712

MULTIRACIAL AMERICANS OF SOUTHERN CALIFORNIA (MASC)
12228 Venice Boulevard, Suite 452
Los Angeles, CA 90066

MULTIRACIAL FAMILIES PROGRAM
Hiawatha Branch YMCA
4100 28th Avenue South
Minneapolis, MN 55406
Web site: www.primenet.com/~dsmyre/mac.htm

PACT—AN ADOPTION ALLIANCE
3450 Sacramento St., Suite 239
San Francisco, CA 94118
E-mail: info@pactadopt.org
Web site: www.pactadopt.org
Pact is a membership organization providing support, advocacy, education, and
connections to families across the country with adopted children of color. The Web
site includes articles from their quarterly magazine *Pact Press*, on-line registration,
and a reference guide to over a thousand multicultural and adoption-related adult
and children's books.

RESOURCES FOR COLLEGE STUDENTS

Racially mixed young people are coming together and forming their own student organizations at a growing number of college campuses. Sara Busdiecker described her group—Mixed Initiatives, at the University of Michigan—in My So-Called Identity. If you are a college-bound person who is interested in joining such a group, contact the student activities office at your college to find out if one exists. You can also check the Web site of *Mavin* journal, a quarterly magazine described earlier, for a list of student organizations in North America. Or you might want to start your own organization. Students at the following schools have founded mixed-race student groups:

Amherst College, Amherst, Massachusetts
Brown University, Providence, Rhode Island
Duke University, Durham, North Carolina
Grinnell College, Grinnell, Iowa
Harvard University, Cambridge, Massachusetts
Johns Hopkins University, Baltimore, Maryland
Michigan State University, East Lansing
Oberlin College, Oberlin, Ohio
Pennsylvania State University, University Park
Ryerson Polytechnic University, Toronto, Ontario, Canada
Smith College, Northampton, Massachusetts
Stanford University, Stanford, California
University of California, Berkeley
University of California, Irvine
University of California, Santa Barbara
University of California, Santa Cruz
University of Colorado, Boulder
University of Michigan, Ann Arbor
University of Pennsylvania, Philadelphia
University of Southern California, Los Angeles
University of Wisconsin, Madison
Wellesley College, Wellesley, Massachusetts
Wesleyan University, Middletown, Connecticut
Williams College, Williamstown, Massachusetts
Yale University, New Haven, Connecticut

These schools have offered classes about the multiracial experience:

Mills College, Oakland, California
Stanford University, Stanford, California
University of Arizona, Tucson
University of California, Berkeley
University of California, Davis
University of California, Los Angeles
University of California, Santa Barbara
University of California, Santa Cruz
University of Washington, Seattle
Whittier College, Whittier, California